T

THANKS FOR AL

THE ENCOURAGEMENT

ROSE

Dragonfly Daughter

The Story of Violet Rose

by

Violet Rose

AuthorHouse™
1663 Liberty Drive, Suite 200
Bloomington, IN 47403
www.authorhouse.com
Phone: 1-800-839-8640

First published by AuthorHouse 8/23/2007

ISBN: 978-1-4343-3233-2 (sc)

Library of Congress Control Number: 2007905864

Printed in the United States of America
Bloomington, Indiana

This book is printed on acid-free paper.

Preface

Thank you to my good friend, Kathleen Fitzpatrick, for her editing my story and for continual encouragement to see it in print. Your editing skills are greatly appreciated.

Special thanks to my friend and author Cheryl Pillsbury she is at fknight420@charter.net. Without her constant and unending encouragement the final steps of publication would not have been completed.

I would like to try console those who feel they have been hurt by my actions. Maybe by reading this book you might begin to see how much out of control my life really was and how little I could do to change the predestined chain of events that unfolded with time. I did not then nor do I now harbor any malice toward any of you. I did not write this book to try and continue to hurt you. What happened is done and over, it is what happens from now on that is important.

Cover drawing by Carlos Claudio at cjclaudio@gmail.com.

Chapter 1

As I approached the cemetery I could see the gates – the same gates that I could not go through 20 years earlier. This visit was a long time coming and way overdue. Twenty years ago I drove up to these gates, and then turned around. I had my family with me then, and they thought it strange that we came so far, only to turn away from the gates without going in. This time I parked the car and approached the gates. The weather seemed identical to that day twenty years ago. But this time the gates looked less massive, less foreboding. The warm Virginia breezes were blowing my hair around. I made it. I'm through. As I passed the gates I could see signs of corrosion. Those gates still stood proud even though time was wearing them down. I was looking for my father's grave. The cemetery was massive and overpowering, white stones marking the graves of the fallen heroes. There was row upon row of stones covering the landscape, so many that the sheer number overwhelmed me. I went to the records department to see if they could help me locate my father. The father who never knew I existed, the father I never met.

Right away there was trouble. The woman at the records counter asked for a name and date of internment. I gave the name and what I assumed was the year of internment, the year he was killed in a jeep accident. I told the woman to try 1950, the year my father died. What happened next seemed beyond belief. She reached inside a file cabinet and pulled out a roll of microfilm, then inserted it in a reader. As she whirled through the microfiche records, I couldn't help but wonder how in 2006 there were as yet no computerized records for the people buried here. After quite a while of twirling through film, the woman said she could not find him. So now, after I had come such a long distance to visit my father's grave, my heart was broken apart again. There was this burden I had carried all my life, and now that I was finally able to face this burden, to pray and ask for my father's forgiveness. I wanted him to forgive me for what I had done and, even more importantly, to forgive him. How could I not be able to find him? Mom said he was buried in the Arlington National Cemetery. How cruel to come all this way, through all those years and pain, and not be able to find my father.

Stumbling back to my truck, fighting back tears, I did not know what to do. I had prepared for this moment all winter. Actually it took me my whole life to get to this point where I could come to his grave. I had a whole lifetime of resentment to relinquish. It had poisoned my very existence, and I had arrived in Virginia yesterday prepared to finally let go of all that toxicity. Today was the day to leave all that resentment behind. I wanted to move on with the rest of my life.

So why was I now sitting in my truck crying? Why couldn't I go to his grave? I was shocked at what a backwards way they had of keeping the records of war heroes. I was angry and hurt that they could not find my father's grave. How cruel life can be sometimes. I was lucky just finding out I was his daughter, let alone to have any specific details of his interment. The burden just grew heavier as I sat there crying. My soul wailed with this added pain. I had to let it go, I had to get on with my life. I had to ask his forgiveness, I had to confess to him what I had done to Phil.

Out of desperation I thought that perhaps I should just look around for him. Maybe for once luck would be on my side. I wiped my eyes, put on sunglasses, and left the truck. Again I walked through the gates of The Arlington National Cemetery, a huge and overpowering place. Wandering the graves for hours, I felt like a lost little girl looking for her daddy. Long rows of gravestones went on endlessly in every direction. The stones not only lined up in horizontal rows but also lined up diagonally, so that as I walked through graves, the pattern of rows changed yet always it seemed that all the rows of stones pointed toward me. I was hoping that sheer luck would guide me to him. But after walking and walking from grave to grave, hopelessness inevitably set in. I read hundreds of tombstones as I wandered. What was I going to do? This burden had to be put down, and today was the day. Could fate be any crueler to bring me so far to this cemetery, and then provide no place to put my burden down? No rest for my tired and aching soul. After 55 years I finally wanted to – I had to -- forgive him, and now the stinging irony was I could not find him.

So I just kept wandering past hundreds of graves, crying softly as I went. It was an unusually mild March day for Virginia. The warm breeze blew my hair against my wet cheeks. I could hear taps faintly in the background, and was drawn in that direction. After a while I found myself at the Tomb of the Unknown Soldier. More irony, because Dad, I never knew you. I found a bench set off by itself at the side of some graves, and sat there crying for a long time, until distracted by the changing of the guards. Again mournful taps were played, making my grief grow stronger. I can't keep carrying this burden; I had to let it go. It just was all too pathetically cruel that an unknown daughter of a hero veteran should be crying about her unknown father in the shadow of this fabled tomb. I know my father existed. I have his death certificate and also a posthumous award given to him by President Kennedy.

It would have been a perfect day if I could have found him. I had prepared all I wanted to say. Why does it seem like fate is always against me? I scanned the graves around me in one last attempt to find him. Sure, it would have been sheer luck to do so, and luck, as usual, was not with me that day. I stopped crying, it was time to do something. I had to drop this burden once and for all. So there near the Tomb of the Unknown Soldier, I finally let it go. I hoped that maybe his grave was within earshot and that maybe he could hear me. Maybe I was near someone who had served with him. Was anybody listening? Maybe only God, but it did not matter. What was important is that I verbalize it all, and let it go. I had to remove the weight from my soul, tortured too long. I turned to talk to the graves nearest me and began telling the story.

Dad, I am sorry that I am not at your gravesite today. I don't want the fact that I cannot find you make everything about today just a wasted pathetic attempt. Maybe it is appropriate that I talk with you at this sacred site. Surely there could be no more hallowed place for a daughter to talk to a father who was lost while in the service. Had I known I would not be able to find you I would have found some place in the woods, dark and deep and private, to talk to you. So if you are with me at all, then you are with me everywhere. Just like Mom. I carry her memory with me everywhere and talk with her when needed. Today I need to talk with you. So here in the shadow of the Unknown Soldier, please listen to the story of your unknown daughter.

I know, Dad, that you don't know me. You died before you ever knew about me or about your son Phil. As a matter of fact, even Mom did not know she was pregnant when you died. I am sorry that in 55 years I never came to see you or tell you that you had a daughter. For that I am deeply sorry. You see, I had some issues, which up until now prevented me from coming here. Your death ruined my mother's life.

It is said that swans mate for life, and that if one dies, the other spends a lifetime longing for the lost mate. My mother was like a swan. She spent her life looking for you, and of course, never finding you. Like the swan, she did not, could not understand why you were no longer there. She grieved her entire life over the loss of you.

I can understand her grief. From what she told me, you were quite a guy. You had two tours of duty in the service – in the Marines and the Navy. Numerous awards for valor, a brave and decorated war hero -- I looked at your Marine discharge papers before this trip. Your list of combat engagements was staggering: Guadalcanal, B.S.I.; Cape Glouster, New Britain; Pelileu Island, Paula Islands. You managed to survive all that. Then how the hell did you wind up dying in a jeep accident back here in the states? It never made sense to me. I can't understand it. At one time I wanted to know all the details. Were you on furlough? Were you drinking with some buddies? For if your death was your own fault it would have given me one more reason to hate you. Or was it just a simple twist of fate… simple for fate, that is.

You were the husband that wives dream about. Mom's love for you was monumental, unending. Her grief was constant and in the end overcame her. You may know that now. Hopefully she is there with you. If she is, please ask her to forgive me for all the wrong things I've done. Her body rests in a terrible place. When she died, I was in a bad way emotionally. She was my best friend in life – we were all each other had when times were bad. She never had any close girlfriends like I have now. Through these years I have learned the tremendous value of support offered by close girlfriends with whom I can bare my soul. Friends who have helped me through the darkness and picked me up after crashing over particularly rough spots in the road.

Mom's grief for you was part of the reason why she had so much trouble in her life. My stepfather was jealous of you. She tried to love him but she couldn't as she was still in love with you. She kept pictures of you hidden away. When I was ten, she started showing me those pictures. Sitting on the deck of the navy ships in your deep-sea diving suit, holding a brass helmet, you were quite a handsome man – a big smile on your face as you prepared to screw on your diving helmet. You looked so rugged and strong it seemed to me that you could have gotten through anything.

After you died, Mom grieved for several years and then remarried. Her family and your family both worried about the new marriage for several reasons. One, it was too early for her to remarry because she was not yet over your death. Two, they did not like her new husband. Your sister Vi was very suspicious of him. Her new husband, my stepfather had forbidden her to have contact with your family, my lineage was temporarily lost. Mom's second marriage, though terrible, produced two children. My half-sister was four years younger than I, and my half-brother ten years younger. Even then after having two other children she still grieved your death. My stepfather was not the man you were. As a matter of fact, he was thrown out of the service on a Section 8 because of his uncontrollable temper and for beating up his commanding officer. Mom was married to him for seven long tormented years. They fought violently. I won't go into all the details, for if she is there with you now, she can tell you herself.

I was Mom's only true friend in life. She would confide things in me that I, or any child my age would not be prepared to deal with. At the tender age of ten-and-a-half, I found myself head of the household. That's when she divorced my stepfather. That is when I found out about you. That is when I found out my last name is really Rose. Dealing with all of this has given me insight into life and deeper compassion for people and their hardships. When I was tested in high school for vocational aptitude, the career best suited to my personality was minister.

Mom was what today is called bipolar, but back then it was manic depression. She probably has told you about how much she suffered. She did okay most of the time. But there was a sinister cycle in which she lived. About every three weeks, she would crash and burn. I knew as soon as I got home that she was in the downward spiral. A pan of Franco American spaghetti with fried hamburger mixed in sat on the stove. Depending on its consistency, I could tell when she had started drinking that day. If I turned the pan over, and nothing fell out, I knew she was long gone, passed out from having started drinking before noon. I hated that pan of stuff, it meant that more trouble was on the way. I still hate that combination because of that association. I would throw out the mess, and fix something for myself and half-siblings. Maybe that's why I'm a good cook today. I didn't bother to offer any to Mom because I knew she would not eat for the next two or three days.

It was a vicious downward cycle. As she drank, she became more depressed. She grieved for you as she continued drinking. Though she didn't call out your name, it was obvious the loss of you was eating away at her inside. After about a day and a half, she would be so far gone, that she would start talking to herself. That's when she became a danger to herself and to the rest of us. I would hear her cry out, "Oh God! Why have you done this to me? I am so alone and stuck with these kids.... Good God, why did you do it!" Sometimes it went on for hours.

It was better to leave her alone than to go near her when she was like that. In this state, her temper would turn on me. If I dared to say anything about her drinking, she would explode into violence. Several times she threw me out of the house. Until I was about 16, I would just go out and walk, sometimes in the woods if the moon was bright enough. Sometimes I sat in the dark, thinking, wondering what I had done to deserve all this. But even so for all her flaws, I loved her unconditionally for I knew through our confidences why she hurt so much and I had great sympathy for her, for a beaten woman whose tragedies in life seemed epic.

Dad, you don't know me but I live in a world of pure emotion. I don't dare go to a tearjerker movie because I cry so much. When I saw "Titanic" a few years ago, I cried buckets when Rose was left alone as her lover and companion slipped below the surface of the water. It's a wonder people didn't grab their seats to keep from drowning in the salty ocean of tears that gushed from my eyes.

So when I found Mom drunk and passed out, I always helped her up because when she did not drink, she was the most wonderful person imaginable. She was truly a Supermom. She would come out of her drunk after about three days. The change was unbelievable. She would be showered, smartly dressed with perfect make-up. Truly she was a ten when she felt good. When drunk, she was in the negative numbers. So Mom, if you're there, I forgive you. But you already know that.

And Mom, I forgive you for the other thing. Dad, shortly after Mom got divorced, she was afraid how we all were going to survive. Your son Phil and I had just found out about you and the Rose family, about the six aunts and uncles and their families. We never knew them because our stepfather had forbidden any contact with them. So one day Mom took Phil and I to visit one of our newfound relatives, and Phil helped with the preparation of the meal. They all talked and watched Disney; they were broadcasting a movie named the "Moon Cursers." I remember it to this day. Then after the movie was over, Mom started speaking with Phil. "You know since the divorce how hard life has become. How hard it is for me to support all of us."

Then my uncle spoke. "Your aunt and I don't have any children."

I could see the words burning into Phil's brain. He knew there was something very important about to be said.

Our uncle continued, "We have been very successful with our restaurant. We want you to come live us. You are my brother's son and we would treat you as our own. We can give you our love for my brother as well as the love we would develop for you."

Mom, Phil was not yet eleven. How could you be doing something like that? You had always told him he was your favorite. For an instant Phil looked all alone in the world. Did you not want him anymore? Then Phil looked at you, and saw you were holding back tears. As you sat there, your hands trembled. Phil and I have always been able to feel a person's aura. We were able to see what they feel. I can't express it in words. But we both could see inside you that day, and we could both see that your heart was breaking.

Uncle said, "It's up to you to decide, Phil." They had money, they lived next to the water; they had a boat, and a nice house. They were absolutely wonderful people. Phil and I could feel their loneliness and their longing for a child. We could feel that love that would flow from them to him. Phil would have everything.

Dad, at that time, Phil could have turned against Mom. He could have lived with your brother and had a happy life. Everything a child could ever want including love. I'm sorry dad but Phil broke your brother's heart that evening. But it just was not to be. Phil and I looked very deep inside Mom. We could have hated her for trying to give him away, but we could not hate her because of what we felt and saw.

What we saw was a woman holding her child above the rising flood to someone who would take Phil to safety. That even if it took her last breath she would hold him up, hoping for rescue. Dad, at that time Phil loved Mom more than at any time in his life. He knew she would not survive without him. That guilt and loss would have destroyed her as well as him, it would have destroyed us all.

As Phil spoke, sorrow permeated the room. Phil's heart was breaking as he spoke, but never there or on the way home, did he cry. He was a man, and men don't cry. Besides, the whole event was so traumatic that it was too soon for tears. Those tears were stored away, put away for a long time to come. My aunt and uncle were heartbroken and sad. They wanted to provide the life for Frank's son that they know he would have provided had he not died. As tenderly as possible Phil explained that he was deeply moved by the offer, but felt his obligation was to his family and to be there to help and that was the most important thing. That he could not go off to lead a good life while his mother, sister and half-siblings suffered. Everyone was moved to tears. But what was strange was that Phil did not cry. They did not notice how he internalized the sorrow to make it disappear, only I could see it. Phil was a man, and men don't cry.

So Phil stayed on and suffered with his siblings. But Dad, in this you can be proud. Phil may have let you down in other ways with his life, but you can be proud of him. He stayed through the hurt, and unlike you, he never got any medals for his actions. No purple hearts for wounds too deep to heal.

When Mom died, I was devastated. She was my best friend, and by the time she died, we had shared so much of our lives, our fears, our souls. We were more like sisters. I always forgave her. That's why I'm still hurting because of her death. I helped her in life and never failed her. I was always there for her and the rest of the family but in her death I failed her miserably. Her last request to me was that she have her own cemetery plot in Littleton.

I know the very instant she died. We were on the way to the hospital in Waltham where she was having her third surgery for the stuff in her stomach. The first two operations removed pre-cancerous growths. The third time was worse. She was supposed to survive, but complications set in and she died. My family and I were rushing down to be with her, when I knew she was gone. I slowed the car, my family looked at me. "She's gone" was all I could say. "There's no more reason to rush." I could feel a gaping hole ripped open in my heart the instant she left me.

Dad, when we arrived at the hospital, she in fact had passed away. My grief was a deep well into which I fell. I had trouble surviving. My half-sister made all the arrangements for the funeral. She was not grieving like me. She never forgave Mom for the hell we had been put through. But I forgive my half sister. She was just not strong enough to love and forgive mom and she dealt with her tragedies in her own way. She never knew mother like I did. She never knew or understood how deeply Mom was hurt by your death.

When Mom died, my life started to unwind. My marriage was struggling; my self-esteem sinking. Like Mom, I had taken to drinking – up to sixteen drinks a day, every day. My life was spinning out of control. I was falling into the same hole, sliding down the same spiral, which had claimed our mother.

My stepfather and half-sister and half brother were insistent that we bury Mom in a grave that he had bought. It is the grave where he was recently buried. He died last year. He wrote me out of his will. He forbid me in writing from attending any services. I'm sure he would forbid me from ever going to the cemetery if he could, confident that in death, he finally was able to break the bond between mom and I. The whole thing has been so sad that I have never been able to go to her grave. I will have to visit her sometime but for now I still hurt too much. But when she died all that was left of our family unit was tattered. I did not have the strength to tear it apart even more. The family had grown far apart, and my life was unraveling. I was losing everything and everyone, including myself. The only relief was in drink. And drink I did, futilely trying to quench what the Irish call "the unholy thirst."

I let everybody down and said nothing. I let Mom be buried there in his appointed grave in Acton. Before her death she confided in me that she wanted her own plot and that she would never rest if she got buried next to the stepfather. I died a little myself inside the day they buried her there. They are both buried there now. So, Dad, if Mom is there, please tell her that I am sorry. Tell her that I was weak and that I let her down. I am still torn apart by the whole business to this day.

Now, Dad, here is the hard part. Here is the thing that brought me to you. It is about the son you also had, Phil. We were born at the same time and as a result we were very close. In fact, we were inseparable as we grew up. He is gone now these past five years. He is gone because of me and he will never walk this earth again. I need your forgiveness to survive. Let me tell you about your son Phil. Maybe you already know him as part of him may be there with you. God, Phil, I am sorry. You were a good guy, and did not deserve what happened to you. You were always just trying to do your best. To be brave whenever the winds of adversity blew.

Dad let me tell you about Phil and his life before you pass judgment on me.

Chapter 2

Dad, we all endured such pain because of your death but no one suffered as greatly as your son Phil. The seed of his existence had been damaged during germination but was still growing in spite of the adversities. A seed does not know it is damaged – it is just a pure life form that knows only to grow. We were born on Wednesday May 2, 1951, almost nine months after you died. It's said that Wednesday's child is full of woe, and Phil's life surely bears that out. My problems were not obvious to the world at that time, but poor Phil entered the world with multiple birth defects. We both carried hidden birth defects that were ticking beneath the surface. You see Dad, when you died, Mom did not even know she was pregnant, and fell into a pit of depression where her health slid downhill. She told me once that her periods were spotty, and she did not know she was pregnant until well into the fourth month. Mom went to your sister Vi and confided in her. We were hidden in her womb, unknown and awash with grief. Phil and I were struggling to survive while our mother had no will to live. I suppose we were lucky to make it at all, and for that I am grateful.

Mom cried to Vi that God hated her -- that her life was in ruins and now this. Along with being a widow, she was about to become a single mother, at a time when it was rare and somewhat stigmatized. After a few more weeks, Mom went to the doctor, who confirmed she was pregnant. Because of the lack of proper care, because her grief had caused her to neglect her own health, the doctor estimated her term as only a three-and-a-half months based on size. Dad, you had passed away five months ago, and because of that the Navy questioned whether we belonged to you because of the doctor's erroneous estimate. There was no DNA testing in that day, or else there would have been no doubt about your bloodline.

Dad, Mom suffered so much. Not only did she lose you, the one she loved so deeply but also now at the height of her grief, her honor was in question. Life could not have been more cruel to her then. You were a Marine, Dad, so you know how much honor means to the soul. She had done nothing to deserve any of this, and I don't know how she survived. But she was brave, and soldiered on, living day to day, enduring her loss and the indignities cast at her by a cruel indifferent world. For a few months she was wrongly branded with a scarlet letter.

Phil was born with a double hernia and stomach problems. He could not keep food down, and was constantly throwing up. Mom said it was a horrendous problem that went on for several years. Life was a tremendous struggle for Phil. About the time Phil became able to eat and digest his food, Mom remarried.

Trouble started right away. We were told that man she married was our father because we were too young to know the difference. We were just three at the time. We never knew you were our father. Our last name was changed, and the stepfather went so far as to change Phil's middle name from Frank (which was your name) to David. The stepfather was so jealous of you, that stepfather could not let Phil have anything to do with you or your past. You were more than dead to us – it was as if you had never lived or existed at all. Our birth records were changed and those records were sealed. Dad, I have not even been able to see them to this date. The stepfather did not treat Phil well. Trying to overcome his birth defects was tough enough, but now he had to deal with other trauma piled upon him. I still remember one terrible night when we still lived in Waltham.

It was a stifling humid summer night, the air hot and still, and my mother and stepfather were sitting in the kitchen drinking. We didn't know what they were doing; all we knew was that they were getting very loud. Suddenly my mother stood up and said, "That's it, I'm leaving." And out she went through the front door, slamming it loudly behind her. Phil was terrified. What was she doing? Where was she going? We were about five years old at the time, and petrified. Phil began to cry and moved toward the door. "Mommy, Mommy" he cried as he ran after her. But the stepfather was near the door, and grabbed Phil. The man stunk of sweat and something worse, and grabbed Phil from behind, wrapping his arms around Phil's shoulders and dragged him back into the kitchen. I could smell his sour body odor and foul breath. "I'm going to raise you!" he screamed in Phil's face. "Your mother's gone, and I'm going to raise you up to be a man." Toxic alcohol fumes flooded Phil's face. "No more dancing with the girl down the street. It's not right!" screamed that man at Phil.

At that time Phil mostly hung around with Jane, who took dancing lessons. Phil wanted to take lessons with her, but Phil being a boy, he was told he could not. Jane lived two streets away in our subdivision and was allowed to come over by herself. She would come by, and we would go out back behind the house. We would climb up on the big picnic table, and she would show us the new steps she learned. Then we would dance on the tabletop; it was our own private follies. I remember it as one of the few simple times in my life. Happy, smiling Jane and Phil dancing under the blue sky. Phil looked so happy. But then, Jane stopped coming by.

That hot summer night in the kitchen, something inside Phil snapped as he was dragged back into the kitchen. Engulfed by primal fear, he sobbed, he wiggled and kicked; terror contorted his face. It was 49 years ago, and I can still smell the stepfather's stink and hear his horrible voice. He picked Phil up from behind, his strong arms clasping Phil close to his chest. His foul breath hot on Phil's neck and ear, he barked, "You need to play with other boys and not with Jane!" That fetid breath was suffocating Phil, and then, whack – one of his wild struggling kicks hit our stepfather, who yelled in pain and dropped Phil to the floor. Phil was in full panic mode. Where was our mother? Frantically, he ran out the front door sobbing and searching. Mom was not there. Phil ran to the corner of the house, and there he found Mom slumped against the wall near the window where she had watched the whole thing. She was laughing. Phil, confused and scared, ran to her. Mom was not acting right – her speech was slurred, her breath foul like the stepfather's. Phil was devastated by her laughter. How could she keep laughing? He fell to the dew soaked grass and sobbed uncontrollably. The stepfather picked Phil up and carried him inside. Other than the sobbing, Phil went limp like a rag doll, his arms dangling as he was carried to his room and dumped on his bed. The stepfather then went back to the kitchen, where he and Mom drank some more. Phil could hear their drunken laughter. Phil lay still where he had been dropped, and sobbed without stopping until the sun came up. I wanted to comfort him but I could not reach him at that moment. He finally fell asleep as the sun hit his face, almost as if the sun had put him back together. He stopped crying and just fell off into exhausted sleep.

Phil's first teeth did not come in right. They were in little pieces and there was no enamel to them. Those little nubs of teeth just rotted and turned black. Children, being by nature sometimes cruel, would taunt Phil about his teeth. Back then a popular toothpaste featured a cartoon with Mr. Tooth Decay to sell its product. It also became Phil's nickname and it hurt him terribly. But one thing he did have, Dad, was me. When kids would tease him and he could stand no more, he could always turn to me. I was always a comfort to him for he knew that sometimes I understood him better than he understood himself.

It seemed like life would never stop torturing Phil, as though he lived under a constant dark cloud. There was never an end to the torment that life sent Phil's way. He began having trouble with this kid at the bus stop. This other boy who seemed to be somewhat retarded, kept knocking Phil's lunch box out of his hand, breaking Phil's thermos. Phil was on his third thermos when the stepfather sent Phil to the bus stop with these stern words ringing in Phil's ears, "Be a man, stick up for yourself! What the hell is wrong with you?"

I knew Phil, and I knew why he did not fight. It was because he simply did not want to. Phil was very tender and did not like hurting anyone or anything. Once again, Phil was just standing there waiting for the bus when the evil-minded boy showed up. Wham, Phil's lunch box was knocked to the ground, and milk ran out from his new, now broken, thermos. Even at that age Phil hated to fight but rage took hold of Phil this time, and he punched the boy in the nose. Blood ran out of the boy's nose as he ran home. Moments later the boy with a bloody tissue at his nose, returned in tow behind his mother, who was huge and nasty. When the bus arrived, Phil jumped on before they got there. But to my horror, the other boy's mother climbed into the bus, said a few words to the driver and dragged her son on board behind her. Phil crouched in a seat by himself, and she wedged her way down the aisle to where Phil sat. Then she slid her bulk into his seat and pinned him against the side of the bus with her girth. Phil looked like a wounded animal, fearful and panting for air. She had that same air of insanity our mother sometimes had, a smell that we later came to know, a smell that came from the bottles on the top shelf of the closet.

She jutted her face into Phil's, and was screaming, spit flying off her lips, wetting Phil's face, filling the row with that horrible smell. She screamed she was going to get Phil kicked out of school. She was out of control and Phil was pinned between her and the window. His claustrophobia intensified and Phil began to squirm. He started staring at a poster on the other side of the bus as a way to avoid involvement. It was a picture of Russian leader Kruschev banging his shoe on a table. The caption said "I will bury you!" Someone had written underneath "Bring your own shovels!" To Phil, that seemed like the story of his life.

He began shaking uncontrollably, and when the bus arrived at the school, this deranged woman dragged Phil off by his shirt to the Principal's office. It only took the Principal a moment to deduce that this witch was as stupid as her evil child. Immediately one of the women in the office whisked Phil into another room. By now Phil was sobbing. He began crying hard again, crying like he had that hot summer night. It was a complete breakdown into tears; Phil dissolved out of control. I was watching Phil cry, somehow I wanted to reach out and touch him and say things would be all right, that I was there with him, that I was there for him. I wanted to tell him that I would always be there for him. But at times like this he would not seem to even acknowledge my existence. Sometime later Mom arrived and went into the Principal's office. Then she took Phil home, where he fell into a deep sleep that lasted all afternoon and evening. The next day, there was another thermos on the counter, and nothing was ever said about the previous day's events again. The boy was still on this bus but now got on at the stop at the other end of the road. He never looked Phil in the face again and Phil would never looked his way.

Shortly after that incident, the decision was made to move to the country. The stepfather was going to build a new house for us in some town called Littleton, about a 45-minute ride west on route 2. We spent that summer commuting on weekends, holidays and anytime the stepfather could get off, going to Littleton and working on the new split level house. We would watch the stepfather frame a whole wall and lift it, pry and manhandle a whole wall section into place all by himself. His strength was incredible. He would lift heavy beams into place and hold them up with his head as he nailed.

There was a boy down the street who used to come by when we were there. He was a tough little farm boy and was different from the kids in Waltham. He somehow seemed stronger. He always wanted to wrestle and roughhouse with Phil. He would not stop until he finally wrestled with Phil. It always aggravated me for two reasons. First, I didn't know why he always had to wrestle with Phil. And second, I didn't understand why Phil always lost as they were almost the same size and strength.

When we got back home to Waltham, everyone was tired and Phil was able to inconspicuously wander off and see Jane. They would still dance secretly at her house but she was beginning to know a lot more steps than Phil could ever learn. Then moving day came, and I was very sad to see Phil lose her friendship. Our half-sister also took dance lessons at the same dance school as Jane. Phil used to be jealous of her, why couldn't he take lessons with Jane? The dance school was having a recital at a local high school at the end of the summer. Our half-sister was in it and so was Jane. This elated Phil, because he could see Jane one last time dancing. Eagerly he waited for the day, since by now we were living in the new house in Littleton and he had not seen Jane in a log time.

When the big day came, we got in the car and drove to Waltham. We had good seats, my mother was backstage with our half-sister, and my stepfather and Phil were in the audience. Then suddenly, we could hear her -- our sister was having a hissy fit backstage. It got louder and louder, and the stepfather recognized who it was. Soon he was dragging us backstage too. He found our mother and sister and we were all hustled out of the school. Phil was bereft and frantic. "Wait.... I haven't seen Jane yet," he said. "You promised." Now, suddenly it somehow seemed like it was all Phil's fault. The stepfather picked Phil up and threw him angrily onto the rear seat of the car. Phil flew through the air and fell on the seat like a rag doll. Our half-sister was no longer crying, but I was. Phil never saw Jane again. Sadly, Phil would visit Waltham again, and there was more trouble in store for him there.

Chapter 3

So we had packed up our belongings and moved to Littleton, a very rural town at that time. Littleton had three lakes. These lakes had once been summer retreats for city folks to escape to when the city summer heat was unbearable. The lots were small and houses had been built that had basically been summer cottages for the first half of the century. Around 1940, with better roads and more reliable cars, people began moving to these lakes to live year round, and slowly the camps and cottages were renovated into houses. Some were nicer than others depending on the finances of the owners and their ability to work on them. When we moved to town half of these houses were occupied by families whose fathers commuted to somewhere inside the route 128 loop, which was undergoing an industrial boom with the beginnings of high-tech. Littleton was a little less than an hour away so it was well within the range of commuting, and Littleton was becoming known as a bedroom community. It was a developing phenomenon throughout the country – people lived in one place, but commuted somewhere else to work. With the recently passed Federal Highway Act, the country was building high quality, fast commuting highways.

But there were people living in town who also worked there, the majority being farmers living with their families in farmhouses. They worked the land that for generations had been their family's farms. At the time we moved to Littleton there were more cows than people, with so many small family farms that the fields of cows filled the landscape. Apple orchards proved to be another thriving enterprise in town, and huge tracts of fruit trees covered fields of unimaginable size. It was fall and the trees were laden with ripe red fruit -- row upon row of trees next to acres and acres of forest. And it was real forest, not just a park with a few trees

When she wasn't drunk our mother was wonderful, and it was hard to picture the monster that was unleashed when she was in the grip of drink. When she shouldered her load and faced life head-on, she was a very beautiful woman. She was brave and proud, yet flawed. I'm not saying that because she was our mother, but because all who knew her agreed she was strikingly pretty. She must have looked very beautiful to you, Dad.

The fighting started again within days of moving to Littleton. But now when they fought, the beauty and tranquility of the woods provided an escape for Phil and I. The natural order to the woods made such perfect sense. The plants all had their separate lives but in living had formed communities where their lives helped each other. The small plants held the soil in place so the soil would not dry out and blow away and that allowed the trees to have a stable place to set out roots and grow. To grow the leaves that would drift to earth in the fall and enriched the soil so more small plants could grow. This was a world that made sense.

We learned to find our way through the woods behind the house. The nearest paved road behind the house was miles through those woods. We had never seen woods like these before. Cart roads, fields, tumbled down camps and shacks were scattered throughout a forest of trees. There were dirt roads that went everywhere and anywhere and sometimes to no place at all. And all of this open territory was without people. It was healing for Phil to go off alone there. There was simplicity in being alone, just to be by himself with nothing to worry about. I began learning where some of these paths went too. As far as Phil was concerned they all went in the right direction; away from home!

Scattered about our new hometown were hen houses. They were funny long structures with wire over the open windows to keep the chickens prisoners in this land of beauty. There were large corn and hay fields for growing winter cow feed. The smell of the fresh cut hay would fill the air. It was a little intimidating how far apart everything was to kids who had become accustomed to the crowded city. In Waltham you could walk to anything needed for basic life -- supermarket, pizza, restaurants -- everything was within walking distance.

In Littleton you would have to eat and drink whatever groceries you bought just to survive the walk home from the store. As for pizza, the only place to go was the next town over. Without a car you were really isolated in your house. There was milk delivery to the house and the milkman brought milk, cream, eggs, bacon and even English muffins and cakes. It seemed like such a simple life. It seemed like it should have worked.

It was late summer, a few weeks before the start of school. The farm boy from down the road would come up every few days and whip Phil's ass at wrestling. It seemed to be a ritual that pleased the boy from down the road. They never fought for real, it was just boys' horseplay but the farm boy always wanted to wrestle and never once in three years did Phil win. Phil didn't seem to have an interest in proving who was superior physically, but the farm boy seemed almost obsessed with it. If Phil were reluctant to wrestle the boy would keep taunting Phil until he gave in and wrestled.

Phil could never seem to get into a good spot with the stepfather. Nothing he ever tried to do would work out well. Shortly after we all moved to Littleton my stepfather wanted Phil to join the youth basketball team. Mom was getting worried about us as we were spending a lot of time in the woods alone. When we were in the woods we were safe. We were away from the madness. At a young age Phil fell in love with a poem by Robert Frost. One of the lines was "the woods are lovely dark and deep." Phil always loved the woods. He had a special spot where he escaped to when he needed to cry, it was a patch of tall white pine. The forest floor was covered with pine needles as soft as a feathered bed. It was lovely dark and deep; through Phil I could feel how comforting this spot was.

When things were unbearable Phil would just bolt off and run there. He would run to his sanctuary of pines, then he would fall face first onto the pine needles and sob. When Phil was like this he would never acknowledge me, and I would have to wait for him to stop, to come back to me. He always came back. Eventually the songs of the birds and the shafts of light filtering down through the thick pines, as though God was smiling on that forest floor, would bring Phil back. Here in that sanctuary of the pines life made sense to us. After Phil stopped sobbing, he and I would brush the pine needles off his face where they had stuck to his tears.

Spring came and we felt better with every day. That's when we fell in love with the country. We found that simply by walking we could escape our hell -- that is, if we walked fast enough and far enough. There were hundreds of acres behind the house to explore, miles of dirt roads to walk. We were surprised by a spring ritual, which is practiced out there in the country. Just before the last of the snow melted and the hay fields were still frozen, the farmer down the road would muck out his cow barns and spread it on the hay fields in front of our house. God did it stink. The machine used to spread it was comical. It looked like a big wagon that was towed and powered by the tractor. It was a strange sight to us city kids. It had a piston at the front that would slowly push the manure back against a spinning wheel that had little metal arms on it. Those arms would fling the manure out over the fields. To us kids, it looked like it was a machine made for only one thing -- flinging crap far and wide.

We were in the third grade and with some extra tutoring from his teacher Phil made it through the grade. Summer was coming and we found something across the street that would live in our hearts forever. That smelly manure which had been spread early in the spring had turned the land across the street into lush green hay fields. It was Timothy grass, the kind of grass with the fuzzy little kitten tails on the end. The manure-enriched hay grew up waist deep. The breeze would blow across the field and waves of little kitten tales would twitch in the gentle breezes. There were two adjoining fields in front of our house with a fence between them. The gate in the fence between the two fields was always open. These fields sloped downhill from the house and were hundreds of feet wide

We used to run downhill through the hay with our arms hanging down so we could feel the kitten tails brush our hands while we ran. The slope was steep enough that you could get one of those out-of-control runs going. Too fast to stop, so fast that each step came in rapid frenzy, demanding attention to our footwork. By the time we cleared the gate in the middle of the first field we flying. Sometimes for no apparent reason Phil would cry as he ran -- barely in control of anything, let alone his feet.

Each field was about 800' wide. About half way through the second field our lungs would be giving out because of the lunatic speed. We needed caution in that field as there were large rocks scattered in the grass. We could look ahead and avoid those few rocks and find a crash landing pad, a place of safety where the grass was thick and there were no rocks to hurt us. There we would finally let the speed overcome us, tumbling forward totally out of control, rolling in the lush grass knowing we would not get hurt. Sometimes we would tuck our shoulders and roll. Other times we would just fall forward like that dive called the dying swan. The hay was usually thick and slowed us down quickly as we tumbled down into its sweet luxurious green. The sweet smell of the grass filled the air as we broke the verdant shoots as we fell. Lying there panting, we would catch our breath and start to roll around and making spots to rest. If we rolled outward a few feet in each direction we could make these private outdoor rooms for ourselves in the lush hay. Rooms where there was no yelling. They were rooms, which had the sky for a ceiling. It was a sky from which God could look down upon us and smile – a private sanctuary, if only for a short time. The grass was high enough to sit and not see over it and, more importantly, nobody could see us. We were safe! Once we had our rooms made we would lay back and watch the clouds. The birds along the edge of the field filled the air with joyful songs -- glad to share their joy with the world. The birds had untroubled joy, they knew how to sign for the joy of the moment. Usually it was sunny, as we would not run through the grass if it were wet. To this day, that spot in the grass remains special to me, and sometimes I still long for that feeling of running full tilt and just letting go, the helpless feeling of falling, but falling with the confidence of not being hurt. Rarely is it ever like that in life.

Dad, one day the stepfather tried to make Phil join the basketball program at the school. That turned out to be another debacle for Phil. The stepfather was a loud, boisterous and obnoxious man. Phil was always very quiet and pensive. The stepfather signed up as a coach and tried to teach Phil how to play basketball. It seemed like such a sudden, out-of-the-blue thing. We had no basketball or hoop at home with which to practice. He just took Phil down to the school one day, and expected Phil to perform. At the time Phil was not a very big or strong boy because he was still rather skinny from the birth defects. Phil didn't enjoy playing sporting games with other children. He was quiet and didn't really blend well with other kids. On top of that, Phil had to endure the humiliation of the stepfather screaming at him, embarrassing him in front of the other kids because Phil did not know how to play basketball.

Phil only went twice. At the end of the first session Phil refused to go into the locker room and take a shower with the rest of the boys. He just was not comfortable with that situation. At the end of the second session when Phil still would not take a shower with the rest of the boys, an ultimatum was issued. Either you take a shower like everyone else, or don't come back. Phil never returned--- he never wanted to be there anyway. The stepfather stayed as coach for several more sessions and then quit in disgust, blaming Phil. He wasted no time in berating our mother about this. What is wrong with that son of yours? From that time on, Phil heard that a lot. Phil could never be good enough. He was still small and thin, and only beginning to really recover from some of his birth defects.

Around that time, mom had the half-sister, and then a few years later, she also had a half- brother. Life was deteriorating for us all. Mom was learning how to drink more and more. The fights with the stepfather were getting worse. They grew louder and more violent each time. Phil would sleep with a pocketknife in his hand and swore that if the stepfather ever hurt Mom that he was going to slit the stepfather's throat as he slept. It was scary because Phil probably really would have done it, he felt so protective toward Mom.

One night the fighting was terrible. They were running around the house screaming, and throwing things at each other. Mom picked up a big purple ceramic statue of a leopard and smashed it on the stepfather's head. His eyes rolled back and down he went, out cold. Phil could only look at him and smile. After a few moments the stepfather came to, with blood running down the side of his head. He grabbed a towel and ran for the car. He spun the wheels of his car loudly as he left for the hospital and he was gone for several days.

Life just dragged on from day to day, fight to fight, day to night. Then one day something really bizarre happened. Mom bought Phil a sailor's suit. White pants, white top with the black piping on the sleeves and around the neck, the little flap on the back and a white sailor hat. It was the first time Phil had seen an outfit like this, and he looked good in it. Lately he had spent most of his time wearing baggy shirts and clam diggers. I don't know where he got them – he seemed to dress differently than the other boys. After a while Mom made Phil take off the sailor suit, and she put it away. She told Phil not to tell the stepfather, as he didn't like sailors and it would make him angry. It was to be their little secret.

That winter our grandfather had died. The circumstances of his death still haunt me and were very educational about the ways of life. Our grandfather had been a weight lifter, body builder and a wrestling coach at the Cambridge YMCA. At one time he had been incredibly buff and very strong. By the time we were old enough to remember him much of his bulk had turned soft yet he still remained strong. As time went on he got sick and weaker, losing a lot of his strength. He had a stroke, which caused him to walk with a cane. My grandmother and he always seemed to argue. One time after his stroke he was pestering my grandmother for something when she turned with a face full of rage and said, "Tom, I wish you had died in the hospital when you had that stroke."

I reeled with shock, what an incredibly evil thing to say to him. I could see that my grandfather was not taking it well but said nothing.

It gave me a little insight as to the kind of hell my mother must have endured being raised by such a cold shrew. Our grandmother and grandfather had moved to America from Nova Scotia during the depression. Grampy was a logger up there before the depression and a real tough guy. Dad, you must have liked him when you met him. They had hard lives during hard times. Nana was a cold difficult woman. I guess she was that way because of the tough times she went through.

For the last few years of his life Grampy wanted them to move to the suburbs and buy a small house. She kept telling him that they could not afford it. They lived like paupers from one social security check to the next. She made sure they lived within the limits of their social security, even if it killed them. At the time I felt very sad for them for they seemed so poor. Later we would find out differently. The truth is our Nana just did not want to leave her friends. Plus it would go against tradition if they left the area where they had lived so long. Tradition – ah yes -- the precedents people blindly follow.

Sometime later our grandfather was mugged walking home from the bank after having cashed his social security check. He was devastated; no man had ever gotten the best of him in a situation like that, let alone be robbed by some punk kid. That unfortunate incident also robbed Gramps of his will to live. The punk who stole his money had in reality taken his life, and Gramps was dead within six months of the episode. He got lethargic; he quit eating and eventually had a fatal stroke. His spirit had been broken by the robbery and Gramps could never forgive what age and time had done to him. All the while my Nana was just as hard on him as ever, for she knew nothing else. What a tragic ending for a hardworking man who had been with her through thick and thin. He died of a broken spirit; I could feel it when near him. Try as he might, he could not hide it from me, and his words were in direct contrast to the aura I felt when with him. He resented what time had done to him;

he resented what he had become. At the time I felt sorry for him and when he was gone I felt he was lucky, his suffering was over. She was such a hard woman that she knew nothing else but to be hard with him right to the very end. What a tragedy it was. I saw that traditions and a failure to adapt with time had left her incapable of dealing with an aging man and a changing world. She also helped to break his spirit. He was so used to being proud and strong and he did not learn how to bend with the winds of change. I learned that even the strongest oak must bend with the wind or it will be broken.

Dad, after Gramps died Nana used to come and visit with us more often. I still laugh at the memory of her chasing cows around the yard. The farmer with the hay fields would keep his cows in the pasture next to our house when the grass was green. And cows being what they are and the fences being poor, the grass, at least to the cows, was always greener on our side. Once in a while a post would fall and then cows were in our yard. It had occurred a few of times a year usually late spring when the grass was lush and in the fall. The house in Littleton had been built in an old apple orchard and the smell of the apples on the ground in the fall was more than the cows could stand. When they breached the fence they would gather around the apple trees eating fallen apples and twitching their tails. We would call the farmer who would come quickly to get them. The cows never hurt anything and if left alone would graze near the trees closest to fallen fence, and be there when the farmer came to shoo them back and mend the fence.

The fence came down early one morning when our grandmother was visiting. She became very irritated. The cows were eating OUR grass – as if that meant something! It meant something to her as she screamed "Their eating our grass!" My mother was asleep, so I told Nana about calling the farmer. She was not interested and was going to handle the situation herself. Out with the broom she went. She started yelling at the cows to get back over the fence. The louder she screamed, the more the cows would just look at her with that blank bovine stare, chewing while they contemplated the fury in front of them.

Then she started hitting the cows on their flanks with the broom and pointing to the fence. But rather than going over the fence, they ran a few feet further away and would stop, turn their heads to look at her with the same blank look as before. Nana would run up and hit another cow with the same results. The cows kept getting further away from the hole in the fence. I went in and woke my mother who called the farmer. By the time the farmer got there our grandmother had chased the cows all over the yard, some had even wandered into the woods behind the house.

One day we were all outside in the yard. Mom had been drinking and she had a funny far-off look in her eyes. She brought out the sailor suit to Phil for him to wear. She was teaching Phil to sing "Barnacle Phil The Sailor." She would laugh when Phil would bring his shoulders forward in a muscle man stance and danced a little jig. We were having fun and time just slipped away. We all seemed so far from the usual madness.

Then suddenly there was a dark shadow; and we looked up to see the stepfather standing there. He took one look at Phil and completely lost his mind. He started screaming at my mother "We talked about this! We talked about this!" Then he started clutching at Phil and throwing him around. He grabbed the flap on the back of the sailor shirt and lifted Phil about 2 feet off the ground, shaking the shirt violently until Phil fell out of it and hit the ground. Phil was terrified; he had no idea what he had done. Phil was beginning to shake. Then the stepfather was screaming at Phil. "give me the fucking pants!" Phil trembled with fear. Then the roar grew louder "GIVE ME THE FUCKING PANTS NOW!"

Phil was sprawled on the ground crying. He squirmed to take the pants off and they were ripped from his hand. "Go to your room. I want to talk to your mother."

Phil went to his room sobbing, running inside wearing only his underwear. But he still clutched the sailor hat in his hand, and the stepfather did not see it. Once again, Phil was emotionally broken down, sobbing uncontrollably, without stopping. I wanted to help but he was lost in his world of pain and, when he was like that, he would not notice me. The stepfather was screaming in rage at Mom. "What did you tell him? What does he know? Did you tell him everything?"

Our parents had a terrible fight that afternoon and the stepfather took off again. Later that night Mom came upstairs and called us down into the living room to show us something. There she had some items laid out on the coffee table. Odd items, tattered clips from newspapers and photographs of unfamiliar people.

Her face revealed deep sadness. She was sitting with her hands folded, and her hands would twitch while she tried to keep them folded. Slowly from deep inside her I could feel her resolve. There was something important she had to say and it was coming. I could feel it starting to rise out of her. Something which once said could never be taken back.

She started slow, her voice trembling along with her hands. She started to speak and stopped. She started again and got out a couple of indistinguishable sounds that seemed like words. Then she stopped and cried quietly for a while. At the time Phil and I had just turned 10. We did not know what to do. We moved to comfort her but she held her hands out to keep us seated. After what seemed like an eternity she started again. "That other guy" was the name she used for the last year or so when referring to the stepfather. I never knew what she meant. She would call Phil "her little guy" and then this man we believed was our father became "that other guy." Well, she went on to say, "The other guy is not your father. Your father is dead."

What was she talking about? "Are you our real Mom?" was the natural fearful thought for any child to think in this situation. She drew a breath and started again. "I am your mother but the other guy is not your father. Your father was Frank William Rose. "That's your dad," she said pointing to a picture of a handsome man in a sailor's suit. Then she showed us the things, remembrances of you that she had kept these ten years. Things that were precious to her, things that were about you. There were pictures of you in the Navy, of the two of you at her mother's house. You were such a great looking couple. I hope you loved her as much as she loved you. She had your World War II ribbons and other medals as well as the insignia off your uniform. She had kept them all preciously hidden away from the madman, "that other guy." For if he found these things, he would have thrown it all away

Hey, Dad.... did you know you were posthumously awarded a decoration years later from President Kennedy for your actions in service? Well, you were. Mom showed that to us. It was a world of discovery for us. She talked to us for what seemed like hours. Amongst the memorabilia was a picture of your mother and father. We studied all those things for hours. The other guy was gone for almost a week this time. We had lots of time to learn about you and your family. And also about our grandparents, the ones we never knew about. It was a time of such discovery. The pictures were precious moments in time captured on film. Happy places filled with happy smiling people. Nothing like the hellhole existence we lived now.

Mom told us about your war record and how you were a hero and that you were buried with other heroes in the Arlington National Cemetery. Dad, it was all so hard to take, so hard to comprehend. I loved the stories about your father, our grandfather, and how he was a ship's captain. How he and your uncles had a shipyard and built fishing schooners. About how no one would buy a boat from a shipyard that had not been tested, and so your father would take the ships out fishing for a year and then come home and then sell the boat. How he would be home for a few months while the finishing touches were done on the new ship that he was going to take out. I have a picture of one of his boats -- "The Kinsman" -- did your dad tell you about that particular boat? It was a triple mast fishing schooner. It sure looked seaworthy. He fished on a huge scale. We saw from the pictures that you like to fish. I take after you in that regard, because I like to fish also and so did Phil. Tell me -- do the spirits of fisherman fish for the spirits of fish, or do the spirits of the fish have filet knives and chase the spirits of fisherman to give them a taste of their own medicine? Whenever I catch a fish for food I apologize to it for I'm sure it had no idea about its fate a few moments earlier while still swimming free.

Your dad sure must have loved your mother as you had 6 brothers and sisters. Mom told lovingly how your dad would go away, and then come back to a new child, get your mom pregnant again, then go back on the boat for a year and come back again to another new child. I guess it must have gone on some seven times.

Mom talked affectionately about your family and how she loved them. About how the younger ones would be helped by the older children and how the family cared for itself and survived as a unit. As you know, she was living with your family when you died. She had fit right in and was happy, probably for the first time in the poor woman's life. She told us she had wanted to stay after your death but that back then there were customs that dictated otherwise. She really wanted to stay with all her heart, as she loved your family so much. But she had to go back to her own parents because it would have looked improper for her to stay with your mom and dad. Tradition!

We talked about you for almost a week. She kept telling us she wanted us to know before it was too late. She said it several times. I kept wondering, what does she mean before it's too late? I kept focusing on that whenever she would say it. Well about a week later the other guy came home. It was late and naturally there was a terrible fight. It was the worst fight ever. Glass smashing, doors slamming, the two of them screaming. Listening to Mom yelling and crying, Phil held the jack knife in his hand, blade open. He was beyond reaching, in that terrifying place we feared for the worse. Was this going to be the end? I thought that Phil would rush out and try to kill the stepfather. But, then it got quiet. The other guy was in his car, the tires screaming as usual when he left. I could hear Mom sobbing, and I drifted off into a fitful sleep. There had to be an end to this.

The next day Mom was drunk. She had been that way a lot lately. I waited until she was asleep later on the couch. Mom, if you're there please try to understand. Dad, you being a Marine, I know you might understand. I did the job with the resources that were on hand. I had always been a clever girl, so I snuck into Mom's bedroom and found her lipstick. I knew where it was because it was not first time I had gone in there. Sometimes when she was not around – she often went to a neighboring friend's house to drink – I used to go into her room and wear her clothes.

I took the lipstick and using the mirror smeared a large amount of lipstick on my lips, and then went to the other guy's dresser. I took out a pair of his underwear, and---may God forgive me if I did the wrong thing but I was desperate; I put a big kiss mark on the fly of his underwear and threw it in the dirty clothes hamper. Imagine Mom's fury several days later when she sobered up and found that underwear when she did the laundry. When the other guy came home they had their last flight. She demanded he leave the house and give her a divorce.

We were saved! I truly believed I had saved us all because I was convinced that sooner or later he would kill us.

Dad, I've got to stop for a few minutes. This is so overwhelming I must rest for a moment. Another reason why I have to pause is that a couple has stopped behind me and started listening to my story. As soon as I became silent they moved on. The quiet was broken by another plane taking off from Reagan National Airport. The warm breezes kept blowing my hair around. I could feel my eyes burning from crying and sat with them closed as the breeze dried the tears from my face.

Chapter 4

The breeze had dried my face and I opened my eyes. I sat there silently while the first robin of the spring hopped by. The grass on the graves was starting to turn green, which accented the rows of white stones. How many tears had been shed over those stones? How many lives of those left behind were destroyed by the death of these heroes? This Cemetery had a very different feel than other cemeteries I had visited. In a regular cemetery there are graves for those who lived long and prospered, those who lived the good life and died of old age among those they loved. The majority of the people buried here in Arlington had their lives cut short, stopped mid-stride often early in life, with families torn apart by a moment of time, families left behind to deal with the dire consequences. The impact of the death was like a cue ball breaking a fresh rack, Lives were sent off flying in different directions momentarily out of control.

As I sat there the guards changed again, and taps drifted out on the warm air. My eyes were hurting from crying. But I had to go on.

Dad, are you ready for me to continue? We'll talk more about your son Phil. I want you to understand his story before I tell you the story of my life. It's too bad you never got to meet Phil. He could have been a good son to you. His life would have been so much different had you not died. He held on to that sailor's hat for a long time. I don't know what happened to it. Maybe he gave up on it just like he ended up giving up on you. He always tried so hard, yet never felt rewarded in any way.

After my lipstick trick, our lives changed but not for the better. I felt responsible for all the evil, which came our way, for it was I who put us out on our own. And as if my life wasn't low enough at that point, one day I got coaxed into the house of someone who I thought was a friend. I was wearing jeans and a loose baggy top. When I went in the house there was another boy in there but no parents at home. I should have turned and ran. I don't know what happened. I remember feeling trapped, they were both older and much bigger. When you're 10 and your captors are 13 there is a huge difference in size and weight. It was hopeless, there was no escape. I could feel their breath on the back of my neck, I could smell their breath. They were saying how pretty I had become. How my teeth had come in nice and what a pretty girl I was. Even now after therapy I still have problems with all of this. I am still stuck at the point of trying not to blame myself, but somehow I still feel guilty. Why did I not run? Why was I paralyzed? I could not even form a word. I could not even say anything. What was wrong? My mind went blank. Even recently during therapy I am still unable to remember all the details. The next thing I remember was waking up in bed. I was covered with a sheet and blanket but had no clothes on except for socks. I looked around the floor and could see my clothes. I felt dirty, disgusting, and filthy, with an overwhelming urge to wash. I could remember them coming up behind me but I don't remember anything after that. How could that happen? What had happened?

When I got home, tears were streaming from my eyes, and I tiptoed past my drunken mother on the couch. I was sick with confusion, what was happening, why did the world hate me now? Why had I not fought back? Why had I not fought off my attackers? It kept going around and around in my head. It was a mess and it was my entire fault. What was wrong with me? It was my entire fault. I kept thinking that only if I had kicked them, maybe I could have run. Why had I not tried? Why?

I never told a soul about being raped. It was my deep dark secret. I only told Phil. Being molested is more than a violation of the body. It is a violation that permanently scars the soul. The young innocent girl I was until then would never be the same.

What was worse was that afterwards, Phil seemed to change. He was the only one who knew about me being raped. He started getting even quieter, as though he had shut down, and was no longer innocent and open to people. But what was worse is that somehow he seemed not to need me in his life as much as he used to. Somehow things had changed him. It was like I somehow had brought us shame. We never told my mother about anything as I felt it was my fault and I did not want her to know. Mom was sliding down the spiral and was out of control. Certainly at this time she didn't need anything more to worry about.

Phil began working out, gaining weight, acting tough. He became very competitive with other boys and started participating in sports. The soft side of him I knew was gone. He would only let me come to him at times when life was really rough, and he could no longer stand the hurt.

We started hanging out more with the two brothers next door. They were two and three years older than us respectively. We had lots of fun with them the last two summers in Littleton. We liked to poke around the Route 495 construction site at the bottom of our two favorite fields, which were next to the apple orchard. We liked hanging out with the boys next door -- even though they were older, we were good friends. After all it was the country, and kids were far and few between. We would scramble through the orchard, checking to see if the apples were almost ready. We loved the apples. A few years before the stepfather had taught us the art of sunset raiding. Just as it gets dark at twilight, when you can still see, you hit the orchard with two paper bags from the grocery store. Fill them and return home under the cover of darkness. It was a technique that we taught the boys next door. They also had a somewhat strange home life. Their parents fed them but kept the refrigerator and the cabinets locked between meals. So these two growing boys were always hungry. Years before when we had met them we invited them over to eat. Mom had them over often and made sure they got lots of food as we had told her about the locked cabinets. They were good friends and we kept them fed.

The food aspect made us very close, and for the last three summers we would camp out overnight. We were allowed to stay in their yard at first but eventually we were able to get permission to stay in the neighboring woods and fields. Surrounded by farms, we perfected the art of moonlight raiding. So from late summer until early fall we would camp out every weekend that the weather was nice and we raided those farms. We loved it when the moon was full as we could go anywhere and see the vegetables in the fields and later the fruits on the trees.

If you could eat it raw, then we ate it by the edge of the field. If it needed to be cooked, we brought it back to camp and put it in the cook pot. One of the deals of being able to camp away from the yard was that when we were in the woods and field's campfires were absolutely not allowed. Our parents did not want us burning the woods down. We respected them and the woods and had no fires. Although there was this one time when we were sleeping in a small stand of trees right in a huge hayfield that was so green the grass would not have burned even if you threw gas on it. There we decided we would be safe with a little campfire. We lit one for a while waiting for it to get dark.

Once it grew dark, we extinguished the campfire, rolled up our sleeping bags and stashed them between some rocks and left. When we can back after the raids we found our fire had not been completely out and had burned the leaves and ground cover in this small patch of pines. If we had not stashed our bags to keep the dew off them we would have had some serious explaining to do.

After that incident, we concocted a new scheme to heat our outdoor feasts. We would buy cans of Stearno, and when there was no money, we found an economical way make Stearno ourselves. We would use an empty Stearno can and stuff a rolled-up a piece of cardboard into it, then melted some wax and filled the cans almost to the top of the cardboard and let it harden. (Mom could never understand why her candles kept disappearing.) The cardboard then could be lit and we had these candle-like things to cook with. One of the brothers next door had read this in Boy's Life magazine. These are some of the few pleasant memories of that time. Not everything was torment and tears, and Phil really loved the fun we had with those guys.

Once were walking along the Highway 495 construction site and, it being Sunday, there was no one around. We found the start of a bridge for Harwood Ave. over the proposed highway. The abutments were up but not backfilled and the steel girders ran across to the abutment on the other side. A wooden ladder was leaning against a girder. Well, we got into talking about going up the ladder and walking across the beam to the other side. We walked, on the ground, to the other side to look for a ladder. There was none so if one was to cross the beam, and then you would have to turn around at the abutment and have to go back to the beginning in order to get down the same ladder. So Phil started up the ladder. Our faces looked up in awe as Phil began climbing. Something was definitely happening inside him. The higher Phil went, the more awesome he seemed, and more importantly, the more respect the other boys felt for Phil and what he was doing. Since my rape, Phil seemed determined to prove how tough he could be, he was striving to prove to himself he was a man. The boy he used to be was fading away, no longer would he be so innocent, no longer a victim. A man had the respect of other men; at least that's what they teach you.

So there on the ladder Phil could see he had instant respect, and it was a rush. Now they were urging Phil to stop. But up he scrambled onto the beam, half-standing in a crouch, shaking, looking at the long run of steel in front of him. The beam was almost 2'wide, plenty of room to walk. The scary thing was that it was about 60' long and about 40' off the ground in the center. So now if Phil walked over and back he knew he would have the respect of those who saw him. It was positively intoxicating to Phil. Phil started off across the beam. In my memory Phil walked across it tall and proud, the wind blowing in his hair. In reality he walked across it crouched down and hands out to grab the beam should he slip, mind rushing, body shaking. When Phil reached the other side he turned and came back quickly, not pausing for a moment lest fear set in. Trembling with excitement, Phil came down the ladder to a hero's welcome. Dad, he must have gotten that bravery from you.

What Phil seemed to get out of the whole thing was that Danger equals Respect? It was the start of his fascination with heights. Also it was the start of what would be a reckless lifestyle that Phil began to pursue, a life that he seemed to feed on.

We stayed in Littleton for the rest of that summer. And when the fall splendor died and dried at our feet, we moved from the beloved woods back to a dismal part of Waltham. It was gray when we moved and we moved to a gray part of the city. We all were living our lives in various shades of gray and darkness. The other guy helped move us in.

It snowed several inches on the day we moved. The house we were now to inhabit was a gruesome old Victorian off Watertown Street in Waltham. It was a dismal part of the city, with once proud buildings, tightly packed together, all of the same vintage and all fallen into the same rundown condition. There were three families in our building. Our apartment was on the second and third floors. It was something I had never seen, with ceilings ten feet high. The apartment layout seemed strange as it was a once a grand home that had been randomly cut up into apartments. I went into our bathroom, where an old style tub sat on legs in the center of the room. What the heck was this? On the side was a rancid old toilet, and an old sink with the ceramic hot and cold handles. All of it made my skin crawl. Not only that the tub was in the center of the room with no curtain around it, but there was no way to put one up without building something.

I felt so depressed. Through all of this I had to put up with the other guy, who was helping us move. By now Phil's strength was increasing and he was helping the other guy move heavy furniture. Of course, by now Phil truly hated him, and praised God that none of the other guy's blood ran through his veins

Hauling all this furniture around put Phil in a good way with the local boys, who watched him moving stuff and noted his strength. When we were about done moving furniture, Phil went out to the back of the buildings and met up with five local boys while the other guy backed a truck up to the rear stairs. The apartment did not have a refrigerator, so the other guy had brought along a used one for us. That thing was a heavy monster - just imagine what a used refrigerator in 1963 weighed. He wrapped a furniture strap around the refrigerator and threw it up on his back, then went up three flights of stairs with it. The kids stood with mouths agape at this man who seemed insanely strong. Never had they seen anything like that, such a show of tremendous strength. Phil learned another lesson that day on how to be a man. Phil saw then that strength also equaled respect.

The other guy left and there we were – in a gray rundown old house, in a gray rundown part of town on a dreary gray winter day. I went upstairs to check on Mom. She was standing in the kitchen, her face was grim, and her very existence looked more stained. "Come on, let's have some tea," I suggested. Nana's solution to a stressful situation was to have a cup of tea, so I filled the teapot and went to the stove. It was a gas range, and I never used one before. I turned the handle and the gas flared up. At the instant it fired it had that singed smell a burner makes when it pops to life. The smell imprinted itself in my memory. I can not use a gas stove to this day without the smell of the gas bringing me back to that spot in time – it would be another smell that would linger in the memory banks forever. When the tea was ready, I dropped the spoon in the sink and went to put the milk away, and wham, I got a shock from the refrigerator. What in heck was this? The ludicrous solution to this odd situation proved minimal---a note on the door of the fridge reminding us, "Do not touch Fridge and Sink at the same Time!!" Ah, the good old days.

When we moved back to Waltham, Phil sometimes used to get into fights at school. He was put into the enriched classes for the kids who had hopes of college. It seemed to be a common practice that these kids in that backwards part of town were considered fair game for the bullies to harass. Phil never backed down from these confrontations, but he also never won either. After a while the bullies just got tired of what turned out to be no contest at all, and went on to torment someone else.

It was a few days before Christmas and Phil was sitting at the window looking out, lost in the snow swirling outside when all of a sudden Mom was at the door. She was drunk and looking to argue. At that moment Phil felt tired and sad, he didn't have it in him to face her. As she watched and talked aimlessly, Phil put on his walking shoes. Mom was developing this ability to argue with Phil even when he said nothing, even when he wasn't in the room. Phil grabbed his pea coat, his dark blue skull cap and gloves. He had bought the pea coat at the army and navy store when we moved. He wore it all the time – it was long and warm. He tried to emulate you for a while, Dad. He was trying to be a tough guy. He left without saying a word -- a dark shadow in the night as the snow was falling and Christmas chimes rang out from a church somewhere.

Mom walked around for hours arguing with the air in front of her. Phil walked up to Waltham center to the park where the Christmas lights glowed, not knowing where to go. Looking at the lights, he decided to walk to Nana's apartment and tell Nana of her daughter's alcoholism. So he started to walk. It was around 7pm and snowing lightly. It coated everything with clean white dust. As he walked along, churches chimed out the joys of the season. Joyous for some, but not for all. It was a regular Courier & Ives scene. And there, miserable and walking in the cold, was Phil feeling all alone as usual. It was cold enough that even when walking at a rapid clip, he could still feel the bitter sting through his coat. It took about three hours for Phil to walk to Nana's. He must have covered at least fifteen miles. I still get an eerie feeling if I'm walking in the snow and hear church bells. I keep thinking of poor Phil that night.

Our grandmother was quite stern and did not really want to hear any of the details, and sent Phil back the next day in a cab. I don't know what went on between her and my mother about it. From what I saw, nothing happened. For Nana knew about Mom's drinking, but ignored it and our resulting neglect. We were to be raised by our mother after all, right or wrong, it was tradition. Tradition again trumping common sense and dictating the tragic course of our lives.

Mother was doing a little better with her drinking but still had dark times. In school Phil got caught cheating during a German test.

The teacher was really angry, and had him come back after school. She told him she was not going to tell the Principal but instead was going to drive him home and talk to his mother. Our mother---Oh, my God -- she was in the middle of a bender. Phil begged and pleaded. "I won't do it again! Pleeease don't do this, please…."

Out of the school they went and into her car. We lived only a few streets away so it was a short drive. Phil pointed to our street, and the teacher turned up Watertown Terrace and then up the hill. She looked around at the decrepit houses, and pulled her coat tighter around her shoulders. She parked in front by the door. We had no car, so we had no parking spot. Cigarette butts littered the dingy hall. Up the stairs, knock knock, knock. No answer. Finally, after several rounds of knocking, some shuffling sounded behind the door, which slowly and partially opened. Mom stood there in her nightgown, in total disarray, completely inebriated. The teacher glanced at her and looked back at Phil, whose bowed head and flushed cheeks betrayed his shame about this scene.

The teacher spoke up. "I… I… I kept Phil after for some extra help today, so I gave him a ride home." As Phil entered the apartment, he glanced back at the teacher, who looked sad. Nothing more about our mother was ever said to Phil by his teacher. The next time Phil had her class she told him his punishment would be to come once a week after school for extra help. He accepted his sentence in silent acquiescence. His German improved.

That winter Phil joined The Boy Scouts, and attended monthly meetings in the basement of a local church. During the winter they planned a three-day two-night camping trip for the coming spring. The time finally came and they were leaving Saturday morning after the leader went to Mass. His church had Saturday and Sunday services. They all met up that Saturday across town at a school. There were two dens going, and some of the boys had their fathers there to help transport kids and gear to the campground. The group of campers included fifteen boys and two den leaders.

Camp was set up in typical orderly boy scout fashion, with two tents for the kids and a separate tent for each adult counselor. They all ate supper and later sat around the campfire – a classic Boy Scout camping trip. Soon it came time to retire, and Phil went into of the main tents with the rest of the boys where all their gear was stored. Phil was just about to unroll his sleeping bag when the den leader popped his head in. "Looks pretty cramped in there," he muttered. "I have room in my tent, one of you will have to sleep there tonight and tomorrow I'll pick someone else."

He started looking around the tent. "Phil, you can sleep with me tonight." Somehow Phil was uneasy about this the whole thing, and didn't want to follow the counselor to the other tent. .Phil wanted to be with the other boys, to be part of the group. Phil had spent enough time being singled out for other things in his life, and didn't want any special attention.

Phil spread his sleeping bag along one side of the counselor's tent, as far away as he could from the den leader. There was a distance of about three feet between their bags. "You don't have to set up way over there, bring your bag closer" the man said.

"No I'm okay," was Phil's response as he rolled onto his side and faced the tent wall. "I'm used to sleeping by myself," he added, trying not to let the gnawing fear show in his voice. Since my rape of last year Phil's self-defense mechanisms had been honed and smote into hard armor. Phil did not have to talk to or be near someone to sense the aura emanating from a person. We both always had that ability. Phil knew at the moment he was not safe.

While Phil was lying there, filled with dread, he heard: "Are you okay? Do you miss home?" Then next, "Do you want a hug?" Now Phil was terrified. "NO" was his curt response. His sensors were on full power. He lay there, trapped, wide awake for hours watching the tent wall. His mind kept repeating never again, never again, Never Again, NEVER AGAIN!! It beat on like a mantra over and over and over. It started softly in his mind, getting louder and louder until he was sure even the den leader could hear it. Eventually the sound of the den leader's snoring blended in with that drum beat, and Phil relaxed a little but his mind now was repeating it softly in tune with each snore… never again, never again, never again.

Phil could hear the other boys laughing in the big tent. They were all chanting something quietly which was then followed by giggles. He couldn't quite hear it. Then it was quiet. Phil lay there with the same feeling of dread he had when the other guy would fight with Mom. Except this time Phil was caught without his knife, which was in his pack in the other tent.

Finally sometime before it was sunrise, Phil made a move. Slowly and quietly, he crept out of his sleeping bag and unzipped the tent. He headed back to the tent with the other boys. It was quiet; they were all sleeping and crunched up. There was a spot in the middle of the tent where there was room, so he spread his bag and lay down. There amongst the safety of the flock Phil finally fell asleep.

When Phil awoke all the boys were up and moving around. Phil noticed some of the boys looked at him strangely. One boy came over, on his face a look of concern. "Did he do anything to you?"

Phil's mind was spinning. What should he say? After all, nothing had happened. "He snores and I couldn't sleep," was all Phil replied.

A few minutes later the den leader poked through the flap of the tent. "Phil, you were supposed to spend the night in my tent. Don't you know a good scout follows orders?" All the other boys stared at Phil, whose defenses went into overdrive, and he quickly responded, "You were snoring and I couldn't sleep. Besides the sun was coming up when I moved. You said I only had to spend the night." The den leader couldn't argue with that logic. Phil's strategic deflection had defused the tense situation.

The rest of the day was fun. They made campfires to cook eggs, bacon and pancakes; and food always tastes better when cooked and eaten outside. They went on walks and played outside all day. With evening came the campfires and the singing and the camaraderie. Then once again, it was time for bed. The scouts were all in the tent arraigning their bags when the den leader came in. There was nervousness amongst the flock, the way a herd of prey animals can sense the danger long before a predator is seen. The den leader looked around the tent. All of the boys were looking off in different directions, avoiding eye contact with anyone. "Not me, not me, not me…." was what Phil could sense all around him. The den leader's gaze fixed on the thinnest and smallest amongst them. "Well, it's your turn," he said as he pointed to the boy, who slowly and reluctantly grabbed his bag and left. As they were walking off Phil could hear the question "Do you miss home?" And then the reply, "a little." Phil felt a shiver for a moment but put it out of his mind because he was with the flock, and there is safety in numbers. Sure, there are still dangers -- the weakest around the edges usually get picked off. Another lesson Phil learned about survival -- stay strong and fade into the middle of the flock. Stay invisible.

They bedded down for the night. The boy who had that morning asked if anything happened was next to Phil. The boy said there was something about the den leader he didn't like. Phil agreed with the boy, but reaffirmed that nothing had happened the night before. Both he and the other boys shared the same suspicion about the den leader.

Phil was not alone in his fear of him. Then he found out the words to the chant that had seeped into the other tent the previous night. They murmured loud enough for them to hear but kept it low so it could not be understood outside their tent.

Mr. XXXXX beats his meat, beneath the sheet, to generate heat, to warm his feet. La la la...

And they all would make a jerking off motion under their bags, and then all would giggle. It was the same thing they were doing the night before. Phil went to sleep determined not to dwell on what the boy taken away might be going through. A key part of the flock survival mentality is not to think about those culled because it only increases your own insecurity.

The next morning Phil avoided seeing the boy who was taken the night before. He didn't want to know. They had breakfast, packed, and then some of the dads arrived to drive them home.

The school year ended a few weeks later. All Phil could think of was Littleton and the woods, the solitude and silence. Maybe Phil could find sanctuary amongst the pines once more.

Phil had two sets of friends. One set was the street rats that were showing Phil some of the darker sides of city life but he also had friends in school he began to hang around with. These kids had parents who were still trying to make something of life. The parents were trying to instill some morals into their children. So Phil and his friends would dig worms and go fishing. I would go with them and we would fish everywhere we could think of. We learned how to catch night crawlers. We got very good at it and learned the tricks. You might think it's easy to catch a worm but it is not.

You need a flashlight to see the worms but if you shine the light on them directly they can sense it and will pull back inside their hole. If you step too firmly on the ground as you approach they also sense that and withdraw into their hole. A worm on the ground is slow to move but with half of its body in the hole, it can withdraw in a split second. You could reach for one and if the worm could sense you, it could disappear before you could grab it. If you happened to just be able to grab the end of a worm, you had to hold really tight and wait for the worm to tire. After about a minute the worm would tire and relax and slide out of the hole. If you did not wait and pulled the worm before it was tired, the worm would hold with a death grip until it broke.

We got so many worms, we had more than we could use. We found a bait store, which would give us a penny a worm. We would collect hundreds of worms when the conditions were right, which is usually after a rain. We then went fishing the next day but instead of using the worms we would sell all of them. Then we would buy sacks of candy and go fish in the Charles River using bread we took from home for bait.

If you took the soft part of the bread and slightly moistened it in your mouth you could form a firm ball with it around a hook and gently cast it out. We had a spot above the dam and off to the side of Moody Street that was partially out of sight of everyone except the Chinese laundry which was next to the dam. The two young sons of the owner of the laundry would come and fish near us. We used to catch carp. We threw away the first few fish until the young Asian boys, using sign language, showed us they wanted the fish. So the early part of the summer we often fished here. One day one of Phil's friends caught an enormous carp. It must have been four feet long. It was too much for the two small Asian boys to hold so they ran and got their father.

He was all smiles and thanks as he took the fish away. Phil looked at the dark polluted waters and thought about the clean ponds and streams of a year ago. All Phil could think about was Littleton and the woods, and how he missed the solitude and silence. Maybe Phil could find sanctuary amongst the pines once more. And then, as if by a miracle, Mom was talking about moving back to Littleton.

Plans were made, and one improvement came out of the divorce agreement, which ordered the other guy to provide us with a car. Mom found a place to rent and we left that decrepit house, and let the city decay without us. But Phil brought along some unsavory remnants of the time spent there. While living in Waltham, he learned how to shoplift with the local hoodlums. It seemed like basic street survival. Some of the kids even went uptown and stole purses from women. But Phil was not one of those, Dad. Phil was an honorable thief, if there is such a thing. Phil only hit the stores.

I need to have some lunch, Dad, and rest. I will be back in a while to tell you more.

Chapter 5

I walked back out to the truck. I had plenty of water but not much to eat, just a piece of fudge given to me by my neighbors back at La Playa in Florida, where I spent this past winter. We became such good friends that they want me to visit them this summer at their farm in Iowa. For they also come a great distance to La Playa every year to escape the vengeance of winter and possibly to heal. As I sat in the truck, my mind drifted back to the past three months at La Playa, and of leisure time spent healing next to the ocean. This visit to Arlington National Cemetery was not quite what I expected it to be. But now that I have started, I have to carry it through. I locked the truck and walked back through the gates.

My bench was still empty, so I sat and faced the graves again. It seemed to have become a hallowed spot for when I talked people passing by would grow quiet and respect me with their silence. I guess it's not uncommon to see people talking to the dead in cemeteries. Those passing by must have thought you were there near me, Dad. Little did they know that I had no idea where you were.

The day was so perfect in every way except for fact that you weren't here. Another jet took off drowning out the taps as the guards changed again. The birds were singing in the gentle warm breezes. It would have been so easy to sit there quietly, and let the sun and the breeze soothe my hurt. Though I could have just left, I had to find the strength to carry on. This had to be completed now, for me.

Dad, I'm going to continue. It was mid-summer and we were back in Littleton. It was like a miracle. We were only five houses away from Long Lake. If you're there, Mom -- good move! It was the best thing you could have done for Phil. Had we stayed in Waltham, Phil may have taken a much darker road in his life. But thankfully we were back to the miracle of the country. The houses were smaller and closer together than the other house we had in Littleton. The lake was our jewel, and became precious to us. Every night the sun would set at the far end of the lake without fail but we would treat each sunset as if it was the first we ever saw. The sun would set and, as it did, the lake would reflect the sky like a big mirror, doubling the intensity of the red and orange streaking across the sky. By then the lake was still and the reflection was perfection. It was hard to tell what was real and what a reflection was and what illusion was. We felt that God had put that lake there just for us. We felt that each sunset was ours alone, as if it would not happen if we did not walk down the street to watch it.

Dad, one thing Phil must have gotten from you was a love of fishing as he continued to fish in Littleton. The lake was shallow and loaded with yellow perch. Phil would wade right out into the lake. He looked so happy and at peace there, with a bait can hooked to his belt and a stringer of yellow perch on an old piece of clothesline. He found that you needed to catch about ten perch before you would get one big enough to eat. Phil built a small outdoor fireplace in the yard and he would bring the fish home and clean them. Then he would wrap the fish in tinfoil with a tab of butter and cook them over the open fire. He really mastered the timing, and the fish always came out so succulent.

During this time Phil was maturing into a man. His adult teeth had come in nice and normal, and he had a pleasant smile. The change in location had brought him many new friends. The town beach was at the end of the road and we spent most of our time at the beach, just swimming and being kids. I used to look at the dragonflies that flew around the lake. They were masters of flight. They could change course instantly mid- flight, stop and land on something, then be off in a heartbeat. When there were a lot of them, you could hold up your hand with a finger extended and a dragonfly would eventually land on it. What strange insects they were, so light yet I could feel their six legs gripping my finger. They would sit there their heads turning and scanning me with their enormous eyes. They were studying me, while I was studying them. Other girls called them sewing needles because of the old wives' tale that dragonflies could land on your lips and sew them shut. The other girls would scream when dragonflies flew nearby.

The boys, on the other hand, would swat at them but the dragonflies were quick. Only rarely was one knocked out of the sky. They are a misunderstood insect, and I wondered if life was as hard for them as it was for us, both of us being misunderstood. Dad, I went and researched dragonflies in the library. They eat mosquitoes and actually are very beneficial bugs. The other thing I found strange was that they live most of their lives underwater. Then near the end of their life cycle they move out of the water, molt and are released from the chrysalis as a winged creature that takes to the sky. They live and reproduce for only a very short time. They actually fly in pairs united as one. I often wondered what it would be like to live a life the prisoner of one world, and then to change and find a life free in the sky, released from the gravity of earth and the environment that produced me. If only I could fly…

Sorry, Dad, I got carried away in thought. I want to finish the story of your son Phil before I go on to telling you my story. Winter came and there was something else wonderful -- Ice! The lake had frozen so clear; it was like walking on a window to another world. Long lake was only ten feet deep in the deepest part, and you could walk around on the whole frozen surface and see the entire bottom, the weeds, some old sunken boats, and even the fish scatter as you walked overhead. Phil got a pair of hockey skates for Christmas and learned to skate well. Phil knew how to skate, but now with more muscular legs it was easier for him. Hockey on the ice was his new outlet, and when it snowed, he went down to the lake and cleared an area to play. He and the other boys had lots of fun at it. Could it be that his life was settling down, that life would finally give him a break?

Snowball fights were a favorite winter entertainment. We would build forts and have snowball wars. But then, one day in the midst of a snowball fight, a terrible thing happened. Phil and a friend had teamed up against two other boys. It was a two-against-two all out snowball war. One of the boys on the other side was strong and smart -- he got all A's and B's in school and was an athlete. He stepped out from behind the snow fort with an armload of snowballs and was walking toward Phil throwing them. Phil kept hitting him with snowballs as fast as he could make them. The other boy was dauntless, he kept coming closer and pelting Phil with snowballs until Phil's back was against the snow fort. There was no place to run, and Phil suddenly was trapped, with panic setting in. He reached for some snow and compressed it as hard as he could, then he threw it with all his might. It caught the boy in the forehead, and stopped him cold in his tracks. He slumped a little, and we all stopped throwing snowballs. Phil's panic subsided and was replaced with concern for the boy. Phil didn't know it yet but what he had done would ensure that Phil would never be totally accepted in Littleton.

Several days after the snowball fight the boy was hospitalized with a stroke. He became partially paralyzed on one side and bedridden for many months before returning to school. His parents were, of course, devastated. Their son's life had been destroyed in an instant, but they knew that what happened was the result of an accident, just normal boys' play with no real harm intended. But Phil took it real bad, doubting himself and feeling it was no accident when he threw the snowball in the midst of a panic attack. At the moment Phil threw the snowball, he did want to hurt and stop the other boy. Phil had aimed that snowball, and the boy's life was changed. Phil was devastated when he heard the news. It seemed to Phil that he tried to assert his manhood, and lost control, and then something terrible happened. It was just too horrible, too tragic an episode for a sensitive youth like Phil to face. The other boy still retained A and B grades but Phil had changed his life forever.

All of this weighed so heavily on Phil. From that day on, he made a vow to never let that uncontrolled anger out at anyone again, ever. He knew that the rage festering inside of him because of his broken life could not ever be used against someone. That would mean no more fights, ever. Phil had already seriously hurt one human being. How could he take a chance of hurting someone else? Once again Phil's spirit took a beating, but he managed to carry on. Day to night, day to night, one day at a time. Only time can heal that kind of pain. I was there often to help him. Phil managed to mostly internalize his pain and tried desperately to have a normal life. His new friends did not hold him to blame for what happened as several of them were there and saw that it was an accident. And we all missed that boy's presence when we played outside. Nothing was ever said, but the other boy's absence hovered around us like a ghost. Life was just so cruel to Phil, sometimes it broke my heart. But I was always there for him.

We took to swimming hard that next summer. While sitting on the town beach one day Phil decided that he wanted to swim to the far end of the lake. He dragged his small wooden boat down to the lake and had one of his friends follow along in the boat in case he got into trouble while he swam. The lake was about three-quarters of a mile long. There were lots of weeds in the lake. I found it a little creepy when the weeds would wrap around my legs as I swam. I hated those weeds. It took a while but Phil finally made it to the far end. He was tired as he and his friend rowed back. The next day he went up to the end of the lake and back. The following day he went up and back without the boat. Phil had found a new escape. He would go down to the lake and do long distance swimming. He did it often. There were really only 3 spots to swim to -- Pickerel Rock on one side, and at the far end there was a dock on one side and a boat launch on the other. Everywhere else there was weeds and muck at the shore. Way down at the far end was a submerged rock where you could stand in about four feet of water. Phil found it a good spot to rest, and just think, and watch the dragonflies.

Soon Phil's friends got into swimming too, and we were doing long distance group swims. Thank God nothing major happened. The only mishap was a cramp suffered by one of the swimmers. There were three of them at the time, and through experience they had figured out that if you got cramps, floating on your back would usually solve the problem. So they floated around for a while, then Phil with his friend started swimming slowly and pulling the other boy with the cramp through the water; and after a while they made it safely back to the beach. You would have been proud of him dad – Phil acted like a true marine's son, his action ensured "no man left behind."

As summer progressed, Phil found a new form of entertainment. They called it parachuting. The boys would shimmy up tall thin saplings and once near the top, which was usually about ten feet off the ground, they would kick their legs to the side. This would cause the sapling to bend lowering the kid to the ground in a fast but controlled rate. Phil loved the rush that it gave him, so of course he had to find the tallest sapling.

It was reckless of him, and it was time for Phil to suffer again. Dad, it was terrible.

Phil climbed up to the top of about a twenty-foot sapling. It was too tall already, and it had gone from that supple sapling stage to the start of a tree. When Phil kicked out his legs, there was a sudden snap. Instead of bending and lowering him to the ground, the top of the tree broke off and Phil plummeted to earth. He hit the ground hard with a thump and a snap, and his left leg was bent back and behind him at a crazy angle. Tremendous pain shot through him. Something was obviously broken. The police were called, and to Phil and his friends, its seemed like it took them years to get there. There were two police cars, a sedan and a station wagon. There were no ambulances or EMT's in town so the station wagon was used as an ambulance. The officers carried the stretcher into the woods next to Phil. Then came the most excruciating moment. They had to bend his leg straight to put him on the stretcher. Phil screamed, blinded by pain. They got him into the car and off to the hospital. The policeman kept talking to keep him conscious during the ride. The stretcher kept sliding around, banging back and forth, and each clunk sending a searing jolt of pain through Phil.

Once we reached the hospital there was another emergency. Our family had no health insurance. The other guy had let the payments lag and the coverage had lapsed. We waited in the emergency room for a long time. Somehow mother had got in touch with the other guy at his job site. He in turn must have made some deal with the insurance agent because a call came in from the agent that the insurance was reinstated. The other guy was a wheeler and dealer. He probably did a roof for the guy or something on the sly as compensation. And knowing the other guy he probably still made money at the deal somehow.

Now with insurance coverage reinstated, they began working on Phil. The time waiting was just a blur of white-hot pain and blackness as

Phil drifted in and out of consciousness. It was time to administer the anesthesia through a mask. The last thing Phil heard was the doctor's voice "IS he out yet, yet, yet...." It repeated over and over until it just turned into a constant buzz. Then later he was awake, and violently sick. Apparently, he kept moving during the surgery, so they had to use a lot of ether on him.

His lips were shriveled with dehydration, but every time he drank water, a moment later he would throw up. This scenario went on for hours. Phil looked around, and saw he was in a hospital room with his leg in traction. My mother and the other guy were there. They informed Phil he had broken his femur about an inch from the hip, and that he would be laid up for almost six months. Phil was too spent to react much; he was still drifting in and out from the effects of trauma and the ether.

That room was his whole world for the next six weeks. He just lay there with his foot in the air. There was bag of water used as a counter-weight, which would constantly pull him down to the end of the bed. The nurses would have to come and move him back. After six weeks Phil could go home but had to have a cast that extended from his armpits to his toes. It had a hole in the front and back so he could use a thunder jug and bedpan. That's when you know how much your mother truly loves you. During that period my mother stayed sober and cared for Phil and tended to his needs. She never slipped and drank and was always there, acting cheerful and trying to lift Phil's sagging spirit.

When Phil was moved home, school had already been in session for two weeks, so he had to have his teachers come to our house once a week for tutoring. I remember one teacher well. Phil's huge cast was beginning to itch, and this teacher had a bad case of poison ivy and would sit here and scratch in front of Phil. It made Phil's itchiness even worse under the cast and he would squirm to quell it as best he could.

The cast remained in place for three months. A week before the cast was to come off; Phil could stand it no longer. He was going to stand up, cast and all. The cast went down the broken leg to the ankle, but on the other leg the cast ended about four inches below the hip. Phil swung his good leg to the floor and stood up. Blackness and dizziness overcame him. He was passing out, and fell back into bed. A few moments later he tried it again but very slowly. So for the last week of that cast, Phil practiced getting up and moving around the room. Finally the day came and with the help of crutches and lots of help from Mom, Phil made it to the car. Mom drove him to the hospital, and it was an uncomfortable ride as Phil had to sit sideways at a weird angle on the rear seat

At the hospital, the doctor used a little saw to cut off the cast. He split the cast and then opened it up, which released a horrible fetid smell that filled the room. Phil gasped when he looked at his broken leg. The muscles had wasted away, and now the leg was about half the size of his good one. The hairs of the damaged leg were much longer than the good leg, as if the hairs had sucked the life out of the leg. When the doctor manipulated the leg muscles Phil screamed with pain. Phil was issued crutches and told that it would be about four weeks before he could walk without them.

Dad, Phil went home and became a fanatic, exercising and stretching that bad leg, constantly working it. He was walking without crutches in less than two weeks. I was amazed at his resiliency and determination. Could nothing stop him? Phil just kept plowing through life despite all the crap that came his way.

The following spring Phil met a girl and fell in love. They ended up marrying a few years later. After Phil's leg had healed, Mom went back to drinking as heavy as ever. All the arguing and yelling was hard to take. And if all that wasn't enough, the other guy came over every Sunday for dinner, and every Sunday there was a fight, and then the other guy would leave with his tires screaming. And us crying.

Phil began having trouble with his teeth again. He had not been to the dentist in a long time. While dating his new love, he was very ashamed of his mouth and would never breathe in her direction. Several of Phil's teeth were decayed and rotting. One of our mother's rants after she got divorced was that we were not brushing our teeth enough. It would be one of her standard things when she got drunk and got tacked onto the end of almost anything "and you kids aren't doing your teeth enough. You better not come to me if you get cavities!" Seems like we had money for only booze and basic food.

Well Phil was getting really fed up with Mom, so when the teeth got cavities he didn't go to her. He had no money so all he could do is let them rot. When Phil was fifteen, he got a job as a dishwasher in one of the few restaurants in town. It was an Italian restaurant and the food was great. The place was always packed. He started there the summer after ninth grade, working for low wages 50-60 hours a week that summer. After three weeks, Phil went to the dentist, and the doctor nearly flipped out! There were three teeth rotted out near the gum line and far beyond repair "Didn't they hurt?" the dentist asked. Phil didn't know what to say so he shrugged. In reality, those teeth had hurt like hell for a long time, a long throbbing time. The dentist shot up one side of his mouth with Novocain and pulled two of them on the spot.

Phil had asked Mom to drive him to the dentist, but he had told her nothing about how bad his teeth were. She had a conniption fit when he came out with bloody gauze in his mouth. He paid quickly and left so her hysterics would take place outside the office. She was really upset, and asked why he didn't tell her. He reminded her of what she said about not coming to her if we got cavities. She just grew silent and dropped him of at work.

It was a tough stretch of work that day. It was Friday and Phil's shift lasted from 4pm until about 2am. It was summer, so that kitchen was hot and steamy all night. Phil thought he would pass out. The bleeding just wouldn't stop, and his whole mouth filled with the acrid taste of blood. But he did make it through that night. Roger, one of the cooks, took pity on Phil and drove him home. The lights were on – not a good sign -- usually Mom was in bed and the lights would be out. But she was up and wanted to argue, and of course, she was drunk. Phil was spent. He just walked by and went in the bathroom and tried to rinse away the taste of blood. She stood behind him, her ranting just going on and on and on until she saw how much blood was in the sink. He brushed past her and went to his room. As sleep finally put an end to his pain, I could still hear Mom talking to herself, on and on, as Phil dropped into an exhausted sleep.

Phil and his friends would take great pleasure in torturing the police. One of their favorite things to do was to take his rowboat at night to the town beach. Phil would go out on the far side of the deep water raft and set off a barrage of fireworks, lighting up the night sky. Then when he saw the lights of the cruiser coming, he would lay in the bottom of the boat, out of sight, the boat being lower than the raft. The police would shine the spotlight over the whole lake. They would look all around, they would wait, and we would watch them from our hiding spots and stay quiet until they left. Sometimes we would have them down there twice in one night. We never got caught, and being kids, we thought it was a lot of fun.

Soon Phil added a new twist. He and his friends would break into summer camp/houses. At the time about half of the places were occupied only on weekends during the summer. They found that almost every camp had a bottle of booze hidden somewhere. The oven was the first place to check -- on more than one occasion they had been lucky there. At first they only looked for booze and left. Then it became more than just a game. If they found booze, they would take it and leave. But if they didn't find booze, they would trash the place, sometimes doing serious damage. They never took anything other than booze, and once again they were never caught. One night they found a case of bullets in a camp. They tore the place apart looking for the gun, and luckily they never found it. That place was a mess when they left with the bullets.

The next day no one really knew what do with the bullets. Phil and his friends were at their far camp in the woods where they always had a fire to cook and make coffee. There was virtually no access to the site from behind, as there were no roads and lots of wetland between them and the next road. Because of those swampy conditions, nothing had ever been built on that part of the lake. It was accessible only by boat. Phil convinced the boys that they should put a pan in the fire and put the bullets in the pan, and hide behind the trees as the bullets went off. To a bunch of summertime boys, it seemed like a good idea at the time. So they went ahead and did it. They waited for a while and nothing happened. Then suddenly, all hell broke lose. They had planned on counting the bullets as they exploded so they would know when all twenty-four had gone off and it would be safe to come out from behind the trees. Well, all those bullets went off at once, and the bark began flying off the trees around them. Phil hit the ground screaming from a mixture of fear and fun. After a while, it grew quiet. Since they had not been able to count how many bullets had gone off, the boys remained behind the trees and agreed that the best thing to do was to crawl away from cover on their bellies, keeping the trees between them and the fire. They were lucky and all escaped. They took off in Phil's boat rowing like crazy and ducking just in case.

Mailbox revenge was another of Phil's pranks. If there was someone in school who was hated by our group or someone who was hated by Phil, they were fair game. It was open season on those targets, and the guys got even with people by blowing up their mailboxes. Phil used to smoke Chesterfield Straights when one day he came up with the idea of time bombs. That summer, there was a guy who drove the neighborhood selling fireworks, and he had the good stuff like cherry bombs. Phil had seen a movie where an American captured by the Germans during WWII blew up the munitions train by putting a lit cigarette in a pack of matches and throwing it onto the train. Phil figured if he put a lit cigarette on the end of a cherry bomb, it would act as a time fuse. Besides Phil didn't like what the other boys did with the cherry bombs. They would fish from the camp, and if they caught a fish big enough, the other boys would put a cherry bomb in the fish's mouth and through it back into the lake. Phil saw this as a waste of fish. He went to the far camp in the rowboat by himself. He started a campfire, lit a cigarette, put it on a cherry bomb and then put it where he could see it. Sitting by the fire, he watched as he smoked another cigarette. The butt on the bomb burned slowly. He sat by the fire and smoked two full cigarettes before the bomb finally went off.

Now a new game of revenge was conceived. Phil convinced the boys that they could use the bombs against the jerks in their world. The other boys were game and they picked out a victim. They discussed where they would put the bomb. One suggestion was the sill of a window, but there was too much chance of hurting someone and causing too much damage. Phil wanted to just piss off the target, not kill him. So he suggested blowing up their mailboxes instead. It was agreed. So the next night they camped in our yard and played penny poker, another of our pastimes. They hung out there and played cards till late and all was quiet. Then it was time to raise hell.

By now Phil was quite good at night maneuvers. They walked a few blocks away to the house they selected. It was a kid from school who was a complete snotty jerk. As far as they were concerned, he was a worthy target. Phil lit a butt from the one he had going, stuck it on the cherry bomb and put it in the mailbox, then they quickly ran back to our place. It was a small quiet town, so it was easy for the boys to see and hide from a car long before it could pass by. They were in their sleeping bags when the explosion broke the still night air. They giggled and went to sleep. But, the next day they were disappointed to see the mailbox still intact. Nothing had happened to it. Phil figured the door must have blown open. He went home and looked at our mailbox. When you close the door, two pieces of metal latched together and there was a hole in each so you could lock it. Well Phil figured if he stuck a strong stick in the hole it would keep the door shut. They waited a week and tried again. Into the mailbox went the bomb, through the latch holes went the stick, and back to our yard went Phil and the boys. Once again the silence was broken with a big bang. This time the mailbox was completely destroyed. That summer of these night maneuvers, many mailboxes blew up all over town. Some of them were blown up more than twice. The guys never got caught. Thank God for that, for little did they know that this mailbox prank was classified a Federal offense, and would have added more to the pile of adversity already in Phil's life. Phil was walking a fine line with all these teenage pranks, but he was managing not to get caught.

Near the end of that summer our mother was in the midst of another deep bender. Phil was starting to feel invincible. He was doing all kinds of stuff and getting away with it. Through all of this Phil was still dating that special girl he really liked. Well, naturally our drunken mother began harping about his girlfriend one day, and Phil just lost control. They argued loudly, and he was going to show her. He went into the bathroom to the clothes hamper where Mom hid her bottle of wine. Phil took it out. It was a new bottle, almost full, something called muscatel. Phil chugged it down, though it tasted vile. He drank the whole bottle and went to his room. A short time later Mom called him downstairs. She had already forgotten that they had fought a short while ago, and wanted Phil to take the car and go to the next town for Chinese food. Now that Phil had his license one of his jobs was to go out and bring home take-out. Sometimes Phil would drive all the way up to the filthy city of Lowell to get Kentucky Fried Chicken. It was easier than fighting.

Phil took the keys and our half-sister whined that she wanted to go. She was four years younger than Phil. At the restaurant Phil sent her in to get the food as the wine was starting to make him very intoxicated. She got the food and came back. Phil pulled onto Route 495 and headed south. He was doing about seventy when it started to rain. The car hydroplaned and went out of control, sliding off the road and into a concrete post. The car flipped over, and slid almost the length of a football field before stopping. Everything but the rear tailgate had been battered, with the roof flattened down and all the glass gone. Phil crawled out. One of the wheels was still turning and Phil's head was spinning. It was weird, like a movie. People who had stopped for the accident pulled our half-sister out.

The local cops were first on the scene. This turned out to be lucky for Phil. The police took our sister and Phil to the hospital. Phil threw up out the cruiser window on the way. By some miracle neither of them were badly hurt. Phil confessed to the police about the drinking. Soon the other guy and mom were there. They other guy went right to work on the policeman pulling the officer off to the side, where lots of heated words were exchanged, followed by quiet talk. Unknown to me at the time, the wrecked wagon went from the salvage yard to one of the cop's backyards. Seems the 350 engine in the wrecked station wagon would fit into a Fairlane with a blown motor that one cop had at home. Phil never got arrested; there was nothing in the paper, never a mark on his driving record.

Phil's grades were slipping a little, and instead of A's, they were mostly B's with some C's. He got sick of having the teachers tell him that he could do better. Their comments were based on an IQ test he took a few years ago. Phil convinced a friend to break into the high school so they could look up the test they all had taken two years previously. Phil's friend's IQ was 130 and Phil's was118. Phil's friend said anything over 130 was genius level. Guess Phil was less than a genius. But Phil sure was smart when he wanted to be. He put the least amount of effort into high school as possible. From his junior year on he never brought a book home from school. He did all his work in study hall, cheated on a lot of homework and studied at school the morning of a test.

Spring came and Phil's girlfriend graduated. She had been accepted at a college in Worcester. Phil spent as much time as possible with her that summer. Finally he had made it to his senior year. His girlfriend was gone so when mother drank and got nasty, Phil had no place to go when Mom threw him out. So Phil would go over to another friend's house, which had a pool table in the basement. Lately Mom was not unlocking the door. Phil would come home later and climb through my bedroom window. And so went this last year before Phil went to college.

During the next 20 years, while he was in college and for a time afterward, Phil did not seem to need me much. But whenever he did need me, I was there to help him. Phil married his girlfriend. It's a shame, Dad, that you couldn't be there. It was beautiful, an early summer day and all of the couple's friends were there. They had a candlelight service. It was very sweet, very emotional. Some of Phil's new friends from Northeastern University attended.

And, Dad, you are a grandfather. Phil and his wife had a boy, who was normal in every way. I was close to Phil's son for a time but now he hates me. He holds me responsible for what happened to his father and he will never forgive me. I have not seen him in years.

Chapter 6

Well Dad, I'm almost done telling you about Phil. So far his life was still going as normal as possible. I did not see much of him for a while because he was off in the male world. He had learned the lesson well at the bridge construction site at Harwood Ave. He learned that he could have more respect from men if he did really dangerous things. During this time Phil's life seemed normal for a time. During that early time he would rarely let me come to him. He was off being Macho Man. I suppose that because of all the pain and rejection he had up until then that it was intoxicating for him to suddenly be respected by men. He impressed many by the things he was doing. Phil had learned well the lessons of the male world. He had spent the time since I got raped building up his body. He now was stocky and very strong. He had made himself safe by learning to be tough and stronger than most men. In being big, rough and tough he felt he was untouchable. If a strong offense makes a good defense, Phil was as offensive as possible.

He played hockey with his friends in college. After one year of college Phil married his girl from Littleton. I already told you about the wedding ceremony. I also mentioned his son. He was born 9 months after the marriage. He was born completely normal. He had not been subjected to massive trauma like Phil had been subjected to while in the womb.

With the male lineage on Phil's side and the male lineage on his mother's side, he was born completely normal. The birth defect which Phil suffered from was from external stress on our mother's body and not a genetic flaw. As you know that stress on Mom was caused by your death. Had you not died, you would also have had a normal family with a normal son. But I guess it wasn't in the cards. When the river card was turned you ended up out of the game. It was very sad. Many hearts were broken and many lives altered forever. But Dad, let's not dwell on that now for I still have a lot of ground to cover before I can tell you about your daughter. Life for your daughter was not easy either. In some ways, her life was harder than Phil's

So Dad, let's get back to Phil so I can close the book on his life. While at Northeastern University, he got the ultimate co-op job, working as a roadman in a survey crew. He liked that job a lot. He was outdoors and it was his environment. It was year-round outside work. What could be better for a man? The only negative aspect was the travel. Phil worked down the Cape running elevations to the water levels of the ponds in Brewster State Park on Cape Cod. They also worked in Rumford, Maine, which stank so bad from the paper mill that Phil called it the armpit of that state. Phil also was in a crew that did topographic surveys along the canals and rivers in Lowell. His crew actually surveyed the area above one of the locks. These have now been restored near the main street and are a source of pride for Lowell. When Phil saw them the locks were totally destroyed and he could not quite figure out what they were as a building had been built above them. You could only see the locks from behind the shoddy facade.

When Phil first saw the locks it was something that delighted him. They had surveyed all the features in the street -- located building corners, elevations of the sills, edge pavement, edge sidewalk, poles, and water gates. If it was visible they had to precisely locate it. The main street looked like any other main street, with buildings lining both sides of the road. Lowell was an older mill city and many of the buildings were showing the tatters of time. Most of the city was in a state of disrepair. Only much later would the mayor start cleaning up and trying to save the city.

Lowell lived in the shadow of its history, having been a huge and thriving mill city. Giant magnificent mills lined the canals that started above the dam and falls. The canals ran to the different mills, and there were locks on the canals to raise and lower the water. The canals joined back together and met the Merrimack River. Phil and the survey crew were standing above the lock just above where the Concord River tied into the canal, its course being changed long ago by these canal builders. All of this intricate engineering was hidden by the shoddy buildings -- shoddy being a word that originated in Lowell.

At one time Lowell was a hub of the clothing industry. Rows of looms filled huge cavernous mill rooms. The mills had rows of large windows so the light could enter and the workers could see. This style of building was duplicated all over Lowell along the rivers and the canals. Some of these buildings were over 1,000 feet long and sometimes up to 6 stories high. Phil would look at these buildings with mixed emotions. Phil was not a capitalist at heart, and did not appreciate the magnificent build-up of the industrial revolution. Instead Phil could see deeper into the building and see the misery of the countless workers who had toiled there. The looms were incredibly noisy and anyone who worked near them went deaf. It was the job for hundreds of thousands of people over time. They would sit at those looms and splice the yarn of a nearly empty spool to a new one before the spool went empty and created a flaw in the fabric being woven. Look at the threads in a piece of fabric -- however many threads there are, that is how many spools there were at the end of the loom to tend. And if a worker was not quick enough and tried to splice the yarn too close to the loom, that worker lost a finger.

If that happened then the foreman would be furious. Not because the worker lost a finger, not because that worker could no longer produce for the mill, but because the worker ruined a bolt of fabric with blood. The workers' lives meant less than a bolt of fabric. The owners of this industry grew rich by spending the lives of their workers. Not only did the workers suffer but they were paid a sustenance wage that guaranteed their continued servitude.

These greedy business owners showed their true colors during the Civil war. Many had contracts to make winter clothes for the Northern troops during the war. Some of the mill owners used inferior materials in these uniforms. They came up with this felt type material that they used for winter pants. They called it shoddy, for then the word did not mean what it does today. The material was so poorly made that it virtually disintegrated while the soldiers wore them. So the owners ultimately found out how to make more money but also how to kill the working man even quicker. For many Northern soldiers died from exposure. And a new word was coined -- shoddy workmanship.

So Phil and the crew were standing on the shoddy sidewalk, amongst the shoddy buildings in the shoddy old city of Lowell when the crew chief unlocked a door to an alley. They walked down the alley not knowing what they would see at the end. It was the ruins of lock number one. Phil was amazed; a canal ran right under the road and buildings. You could travel by this spot for thousands of times and have no idea that you were passing over a canal that had once made Lowell the capitol of cloth.

Phil always loved historical buildings and engineering projects, and here he was standing at historical ruins. As roadman it was his job to walk and crawl around those abandoned abutments of a once grand highway of water. He would bring the survey rod to all of the spots, making measurements so that a comprehensive drawing could be done at the home office.

Later the survey crew would traverse the banks of Lowell's rivers, locating every detail they saw. It was like taking a picture of one leaf, one blade of grass at a time. Down the banks of the Merrimack River they worked. At the time the river was a mess. Strands of toilet paper and condoms hung from the branches just above the water. Every once in a while a tampon would float by like a big sperm on its way to the fertile sea. This job lasted six months and then it was back to school. At this time, Dad, Phil's wife was pregnant with your grandson, and a few months later your grandson was born, a normal strapping boy in every way. You would have loved him, Dad, had you been able to meet him. Phil loved him with all his heart. The boy was Phil's pride and joy, and at first they were the best of friends.

After the next quarter of school was over the placement office called Phil to come to the office. The company he had worked for did not need workers this quarter. Phil told the counselor that he now had a son and needed to make as much money as possible. The counselor thought for a minute and asked Phil. "Are you afraid of heights?" Phil thought about the Harwood bridge crossing and also all the roofs and staging he had worked on with a local builder before going to college. He had worked on all of this stuff without fear so Phil answered "No." Phil was given an address in Lowell to go for an interview, back to the city of shod.

Dad, I need to back up for a moment. I'm sorry, Dad, the memories seem to get jumbled sometimes. So far college had been very tough for Phil but he made it through. The freshman year was particularly hard. Not only did Phil's poor study habits catch up with him, but in 1970, his freshman year, the city of Boston and its colleges were being torn apart by student riots and protesting. The Vietnam war was still raging and the students of the world were rallying to try and stop the killing.

Also Phil was struggling with what was then called "life or death academics." The year he had gone to college was the last year they gave out student deferrals. The government had started a lottery of death. They randomly drew birthdays and arranged a chart of death according to birthdays 1-365. Then they would start at one and draft the boys who had birthdays on that chart. Phil's number was 38. Every year they would do the draft again for the boys who turned 18 and that was the number you kept. The first year Viet Nam deployments went up almost to number 200. Had Phil flunked out of school, he surely would have been drafted and gone to Viet Nam.

For several years before college Phil had opposed the war. He just did not see the threat to our country. We were fighting a backward nation with no technology in a country with jungles and lots of cover that provided hiding places from which to attack. Unless we laid waste to the entire country, killed all the vegetation, killed all the people and shot anything that moved; we could never win. But what really turned Phil against the war was that even in South Vietnam, the side we were fighting for had only fifty percent support from the native people. So here we are in a country fighting a civil war with marginal support from the side we were on. So why were we even there?

The right wing would parade out all the same patriotic stuff from previous wars and we were supposed to just blindly follow it. These politicians used scare tactics, like "We have to stop the spread of communism in that area. Before you know it they'll be invading Australia." But this made no sense. Were the Viet Cong going to paddle their sampans across the ocean to get there? Also many US citizens still resented the McCarthy era and all that blacklisting crap. Many were beginning to realize that it was an ominous time and that our civil rights had been violated by what went on with McCarthy. That Americans were now losing rights and freedoms because of the government, and that the government which was set up to ensure our rights, was slowly taking them away. McCarthy and his followers would have created a new world for us if they could, and life in America would have been pretty grim. As it was, they were allowed to go altogether too far with what they did.

It was a very pivotal time in American history. Phil still felt that if nothing else our generation helped to save the American way. That if the rioters and protesters had not helped change the course of history, that people in this country would now have less rights than the countries accused of repressive governments.

It was a very exciting time to be in the city of Boston. It would have been educational if Phil had more free time to participate. But academically he was fighting for his life. Several times when the dorm room was empty, he would lay in his bed with the lights out crying quietly, if anyone came in he would just act like he was sleeping. He hurt for himself, he hurt for the world. His heart was just too tender for a man living in a cruel world.

At school there were student protests, buildings being occupied, riots, marches, bomb threats. It seemed at least once a day they would have to evacuate a building while the bomb squad searched. One week things took a really violent turn. Classes were canceled without notice. All week there had been crowds outside the dorm, and car windows were being broken. Phil could sense things, something was going to happen. He convinced two of his roommates, whose homes were far away, to leave that day and come to Littleton with him. His intuition proved right as that night there was a riot in the street with people in his dorm throwing stuff out the windows. The swat team invaded his dorm and went into all the rooms that faced the street and beat the kids up. One kid walked with a cane for several weeks after he was clubbed. Phil's room faced the street but luckily it was unoccupied.

Another thing Phil discovered at school was drugs. In their dorm apartment there was an instant division among the residents. Two of the kids looked like refugees from Woodstock and the rest of them had short hair and a preppy look. There were three rooms to their dorm. One room had a door that closed and they stuck the Woodstock crowd in there. They could smell the incense and hear their music.

One day one of the stoners left two joints in the bathroom. One of the other boys found it and immediately turned it over to the student advisor on our floor. When Phil heard about it, he felt that we should have dealt with this first incident among ourselves rather than running straight away to the authorities. But the other kids were really angry with the stoners, and feared their education was at stake and we all could be thrown out of school.

At first the stoners seemed like they were in trouble but it turns out that they had put two hand rolled tobacco cigarettes in the bathroom to see what would happen. It was just a big joke. The authorities took it seriously but the stoners said that they simply like to roll their own cigarettes and did not know what all the fuss was about so the whole incident was dismissed. The other kids were pissed off, but Phil was kind of amused by it. Maybe the stoners were not as stupid as the other kids thought. They sure had pulled a crafty joke on all of them, and Phil definitely had a prankster side. Sometime later when only the stoners and Phil were in the dorm, Phil went into their room to tell them that even though he thought that what had happened was not cool, the outcome was funny. They all talked and became friendly. Sometime later when Phil was going out the door on his way home for the weekend one of the stoners offered Phil a joint. Phil took it with him.

Now Phil had a new friend to help him through his rough spots. For a long, long time Phil never needed me to come and comfort him. When life got tough Phil escaped by getting stoned. Phil took to pot like a bird takes to the air. When not studying Phil was off traveling. Flying to the far corners of his mind. Between alcohol and pot he found a way to block the pain.

Phil smoked his first joint with Tom, a soldier who was staying with the parents of Phil's future wife. They both liked what they felt and decided to get more. Phil and Tom became friends. When Phil did not have to study, they shared gin lemon sevens – a shot of gin, a lemon slice, and Seven-Up. It had a way of cleaning the taste of the joint out of their mouths after they smoked one. Phil was happy, he was high. The ugly string of events that made up his youth was just this soft buzz in the background.

Phil would let Tom down when, a few months later, Tom's orders were to go to Viet Nam. Naturally, Tom was afraid and did not want to go. In order to evade deployment, Tom stole a syringe of morphine from the hospital in Fort Devens where he was stationed, and approached Phil with a strange proposition. Tom wanted Phil to break his arm. He only had 6 more months in the army and a broken arm would prevent him from ever going to Viet Nam.

Tom had all the details worked out. One night when Phil's future in-laws were not home, Tom laid out two pieces of firewood on the ground and brought out a huge five-foot steel pry bar. Tom shot the morphine into the muscles around his forearm. He told Phil he did not want to hit a vein as he wanted the full effect of the drug to be on the arm. Phil and Tom smoked a joint and drank gin lemon sevens until Toms arm was numb. Tom then explained the plan to Phil.

"I'm going to lie on the ground and put my forearm between the logs. I want you to take the heavy bar, lift it high and bring it down hard and break the arm."

Phil was repulsed but reluctantly agreed. He raised the bar and started down with it. But the image of the boy crippled by a snowball flashed though Phil's haze, and at the last minute, he pulled back. He could not stop the blow but he softened it enough that it did not break Tom's arm. Instead the next day when Tom sobered up he found just a huge painful bruise. Tom was angry at Phil for not completing the job, and went off to Viet Nam three days later. Phil was sad because he had let a friend down. But Tom had shown Phil how drink could erase a painful memory.

Well Dad, I want to go back to where I was a minute ago. I'm sorry, Dad, if this is a little hard to follow but my memory of things comes back to me in clumps and is not always sequential. But you have plenty of time to listen. Phil went up to Lowell for the interview for his next job.

Phil's interview was set up in Lowell at one of the job sites. Lowell University was building two eighteen-story dormitories. Phil arrived and met with his future boss, who hustled them into the work elevator and up to the upper levels where Phil would work. They were up about twelve floors and he wanted Phil to go to the edge with him to look at the view. This floor had just been recently poured and opened up for work. There was a floor and a ceiling and nothing else. No walls! Phil's job would be to set a transit up on the floor and layout where the wall panels where to be hung on the exterior of the building. They were pre-cast concrete panels that bolted onto the sides of the building as the exterior walls. Once these were in place the floor would be ready for HVAC, plumbers and electricians. So once the floor was poured it was always a push to get the panels up. The boss explained that if this aspect of the job fell behind the whole project fell behind.

For this interview Phil's future boss insisted that they walk right to the edge of the floor and look out at the view. He said the view was one of the benefits of the job. So they stood with their feet right at the edge of the floor and gazed out at the Merrimack River. It was breathtaking. Everything has a way of looking so clean from above. The Merrimack River was meandering past them, the sun glistening off the water. It looked so clean and blue to Phil. He was amazed at how beautiful Lowell looked at that height. It did not resemble the shoddy Lowell he had seen at ground level. At one time Phil's new boss was pointing out stuff on the ground, insisting that Phil lean out and look down at these things. They were over one hundred feet up. One hundred feet on the ground may seem like nothing, but make it a vertical one hundred feet and it is something.

Phil was nervous, but he could do what his boss wanted. He found later that even if you work heights for a long time and then don't do it for a while, that it takes a week or two to get your legs back. So Phil, even though shaky, passed the interview and had the job. The first day on the job Phil learned something about vertical work. When he left for work it was an early spring day with a forecast for temps in the fifties. He left dressed for a spring day -- dungarees, shirt and denim jacket, plenty warm enough for survey. But Phil was freezing on his new job as both the temperature and wind chill factor went down very quickly the higher you went. You can be warm and toasty on the ground but up a few floors the wind chill can be punishing

That co-op work quarter went by quickly. It took a week or two but Phil was comfortable working and living on the edge and he really liked it. It was life and death thrill work and he was getting paid to do it. He was feasting on it mentally, king of the hill, what a man! When he told his fellow students about the job they would all gasp.

Soon Phil was back in school and had made enough money for his family to survive. This quarter went by quickly and his grades were slowly getting better. He had three friends with whom he had grown close to. They worked out a homework study group. They would get a study room and then split the homework up. If there were twenty problems they would get five problems each. They would work out their assigned problems and then share and explain their solutions and where in the books the answer came from. It really was an effective way to study. They would all get good homework grades and it prepared them for the tests as they better understood the materials. All of their grades improved dramatically. Ethically they were supposed to be doing all of the problems by themselves but they were learning how to be engineers and they figured a way that was much shorter and very much more effective for learning.

The next co-op quarter of work for Phil was near Harvard Square working on a building for Harvard University. It was the same kind of work that he did in Lowell. But now, more and more his time off was filled with heavy drinking and smoking pot on a regular basis. The timed passed quickly and then it was back to school. Things in his life were simple. Work, study, work, study, the routine made time pass quickly. After this quarter in school Phil's boss had a substantial project for him. Phil had a six-month period to work and he was assigned to the Tufts Dental Tower in downtown Boston. It was to be different than the last two jobs. The last two jobs were cast-in-place concrete, which means that each floor was formed up and concrete pumped up to the reinforced walls and floors, and that made the structure. This new building was different in the fact that it was open steel construction. Vertical steel beams go up and the floor steel is bolted and welded onto the verticals. This floor steel then had trusses and a thinner concrete floor poured on top. The result is a much lighter building that was built on piles driven deep into the soft Boston soil. That area was known for what is called "Boston Blue Clay." Buildings not built on piles would settle and crack. But the big difference for Phil was that he had to start going out on just the steel girders, without a floor. The job involved walking the open steel beams.

If working in Lowell had been a rush, then this was just mind boggling. Phil had an iron worker assistant and a huge set of plans. This job he really liked. The engineer before him had not gone out on the steel and relied on his assistant iron worker to walk out onto the steel. So when Phil started the steel workers assumed he was another one of those sissy engineers. But right away they saw things were different. Phil trained his assistant to use the transit and Phil himself went out on the steel to make the marks for construction. This earned him the instant respect of all the workers on the site. Phil got in good with the iron workers and would have the morning coffee break with them everyday.

Phil was a man amongst men, or so he thought. One of the macho games played at morning coffee was cruel but probably necessary. The iron workers had a kid apprentice who really should not have been on the site. He was afraid of heights! Their daily game was to send him for coffee and when he came back they would all be in different parts of the steel beams, and the kid would have to take a step or two on out on the steel beams to give the workers their coffee. It was a cruel game, and the iron workers would laugh and make fun of the kid. But on the other hand his fear made him useless, and he should not have been there. It was one thing if you got hurt from your own actions, but it was unforgivable if someone else got hurt because of your actions. This kid not only was a danger to himself but those around him. If he fell on someone, that person would die.

Phil and his assistant Tim became good friends, and developed a daily routine. As engineers, they were expected to be at that site one hour before the iron workers started. They were also to stay at least one hour after the iron workers left at the end of the day. As a result they were first to arrive and last ones to leave everyday. When the weather permitted -- you can't climb wet steel -- they would climb to the highest point on the steel constructed that day after all the iron workers left and smoke a joint. After getting high they would look out at the city stretched out below them. It was downtown Boston and there was plenty to see. The evening rush hour clogged the streets below. But there were Phil and Tim flying high above the throng. They were on one of the highest points around and the view was thrilling. After getting stoned and sitting on their lofty thrones, which they called the nest, they would climb down. Afterwards they would drive back to Tim's house in Cambridge, drinking Wild Irish Rose. Phil would pick him up every morning as parking at the construction site was very tight, and only one spot was allowed for the two of them. After a while they were not just smoking at the end of the day but they were smoking on the way to work. Soon they were finding places where the wind blew right to disperse a fragrant smoky trail, and they were getting stoned throughout the day.

Dad, I don't know how Phil did it, but his grades improved in school. By the time he graduated from Northeastern he was making Dean's list. He became the engineer and surveyor he had always wanted to be. Eventually he started his own business and had the respect of other surveyors and businessmen. His life for a while looked like he had finally been given a break.

So Dad, for a while Phil believed that he had made it, and that his life was finally under his control. He had a wife and son. He had a house in the country, new cars and trucks. On the outside it looked like the average American family. Phil was working hard at his profession and had the respect of others.

At one job he had as survey crew chief, he trained every new person hired to work in the field. Many of them went on to make surveying a career. Phil would be one of their sponsors when it came time for recommendations to the Board of Registration. They all made it as Phil had trained them well. They make their living using the training and work ethics that Phil had instilled into them during their training.

Phil continued plowing through life. He avoided his past by drinking more and more. At work he never drank, so professionally he never had any issues. Outside of work Phil drank like a fish. But when Phil drank and was with people he was a fun-filled party boy and everyone loved to have him around.

When Phil drank at home alone he was pensive and quiet. So stoic was Phil that his wife never really knew how much he was drinking. Phil was managing to control his birth defects and seemingly have a normal life for a while, but Phil was drinking an ever increasing amount of alcohol each day.

After Phil's son was grown and out of the house for a few years, Phil got a boat large enough for the ocean. During this time Phil met a new friend Jack. They became the best of friends. They were in the same bowling league and hung out almost daily. Jack would come by Phil's office at the end of the day with rum and coke. They would sit and drink and plan the next ocean fishing trip. By now Phil was a registered land surveyor and was running a business of his own with a nice office out behind his house. The office was becoming a place where almost daily friends would come by to drink. People were there partying almost every day of the week after work.

Jack was becoming a problem for Phil. Jack drank even more than Phil and wanted Phil to keep up with him. Jack liked how fun and silly Phil would get when he was drunk so Jack kept pouring long after Phil would have stopped if on his own. It made Jack happy to be able to control Phil like that, as if Phil's job was to amuse him.

Phil and Jack would take the boat out whenever the conditions were safe enough. They would go about 25 miles out to sea to a place called Jeffrey's Ledges and fish. It was 10 miles out beyond the range of their marine radio but they didn't care. It seemed like there wasn't anything on the ocean that they couldn't handle with booze and balls.

There they sat in opposite corners in the back of the boat. There was a huge marine cooler between them. The boat would rise with the wave and come back down into the trough. The ice in the glasses of rum and coke would jingle each time in the holders. The intense sun would bake the entire boat and made for thirsty times. Sometimes the cooler would be so full of fish it wouldn't close. Many trips yielded over 50 pounds of fillets.

Phil would stop drinking on the way in. The dock was always a hub of activity with boats being launched or pulled out along with people just watching the activity. Also many times there was fish and game officers checking on people and boats. It would not have been appropriate to step from the boat to the dock and fall on one's face because of alcohol. So Phil kept it together for that and the long ride home towing the boat.

It was the type of life that many men would envy. With the abuse of his childhood way behind him, Phil seemed to have it all. He had guided himself into the good life. So what was his problem? Well Dad, his problem was me.

Chapter 7

Daddy, I have to tell you about myself before we go on. It may be difficult to understand so please be patient. I was there with your son Phil right from the start. As a matter of fact your son never really existed. There was a physical body which was in fact your biological son but what was inside was never your son. What was inside was me, your daughter. Something happened in Mom's womb when you died. She could not have been pregnant for more than a couple of weeks when you were killed. The trauma overwhelming her was also happening to me, unknown and tucked away in her womb. Something happened, something permanent.

I knew right from the start that I was not quite like the other boys. When I was really young, it did not matter. I was an innocent child and was free to express myself. I liked to wear clothes that were androgynous. From about the age of six or so I would enjoy sneaking off and playing with my mother's clothes, and eventually that turned into wearing them.

I had a hard time dealing with boys right from the start. I really didn't understand them. But when I was young it didn't matter. As I got a little older, my parents were concerned because most of my friends were girls. As I told you my home life was really wretched. So I tried to act the role in life into which I was cast, and play the roll of son as best as I could. But when life was so cruel, and the role of Phil was too tough to continue, I would retreat to the central core of my existence, which had always been female. There I could be me. Like the woods it all made sense -- there was harmony in that central core. I was just starting to learn how to cultivate that core and how to start to bring it to the surface when my childhood innocence was ripped away.

The crushing blow was the rape. I was raped for being Violet Rose. The shame and the pain were unbearable. I vowed that something like that would never happen again. That's when I began fabricating that person the world came to know as Phil.

After the rape I buried the soft side very deep. I would only show my femininity under extreme conditions and only in secrecy away from the world. I built this hard shell to protect me. I began working out with weights to try and bulk up. I tried to be the tough guy. I took on an image of what I thought I needed to be, and tried to bury Violet deep in the back of my mind and make her go away. But she just would not go away. For it was Violet who was real; Phil was the imposter. Yet it was always Phil who was seen in public.

When I was younger I had strange dreams about somehow becoming a woman. In my dreams I was always grateful to have become a woman. The dream was always in the same hospital somewhere far away from the world. When I awoke I seemed to be in a state of bliss that was always instantly vaporized by reality. So I worked hard at building the shell I was creating – this person, which I would present to the world. But whenever the life of Phil became overpowering I would always find solace in the true core of my existence.

It was almost like some kind of bulimia of the mind. When I had too much of reality and could not take it any more, I would sneak off to the restroom in my mind and purge. Once purged and bathing in what seemed to be some the healing light from the central core, I would feel somewhat better and could return to the world of Phil to continue to carry his load. And as is usually the case with bulimia, I could never admit my affliction to anyone.

After returning to the life of Phil, I would then bury the incident in that pit where you throw stuff in the back of the mind. The pit with the sign "unresolved issues" and there it sits to eat away at you slowly, like some kind of rust of the soul. At first it spreads ever so gradually, starting off in the cracks unseen, unknown. Then it starts to tarnish the surface, and with time destroys the vessel into which it was put and allowed to grow. Because all along as the vessel weakens it is still being filled by more stuff to be stored rather than faced. It is just a matter of time before something has to give. But in some ways, it is a normal to bury issues because it is a survival function for many people because life can throw things at you more quickly than you can deal with them.

When I reached puberty it was easier to make this male shell more believable. My muscles grew, my voice deepened and I was becoming covered with nasty body hair. I hated the stuff. I still could not quite figure things out and life was throwing stuff at me too quickly. All during my teenage years when life was too tough, I would sneak off in my mind and purge. Hide it all, and then go back to Phil's life. For a while I tried very hard to be Phil. I really believed that I could make it all work. For a while it did work, and I lived seemingly safe in that shell. I studied the ways of boys and men in order to make my performance believable. So I got through those terrible years at home and headed for college. By now the testosterone was pumping full strength as the biological part of me continued on its pre-programmed journey.

I still did not understand Violet and tried to purge her from my life several times. Acceptance had not come yet so Violet and Phil were somehow all twisted up, still somehow vainly trying to be one and at peace, but it was impossible.

Later on in life, my dream changed and became dark and sinister, like a scary science fiction movie. It started off in a concrete parking garage, where I was being pursued by a deadly enemy. The incoming fire from the unseen enemy was damaging the things around me. At the time the dreams started, I was married and had a child, and my family was always in the dream. When I awoke the dream was still vivid and I could remember every detail of the nightmare. When I fell asleep, the dream would often return and pick up from where it left off. It was an ongoing war. My family and I would be always on the run while what seemed like World War III exploded around us.

In the dream, we were running through burning cities, and trying to hide in houses as nuclear blasts lit the sky in the distance. We were always on the run, always just a few steps ahead of the unseen pursuers. After a while I just resigned myself to having these dreams. They did not occur nightly because I was developing into a full-blown alcoholic and many nights I simply passed out into a dreamless state after drowning myself with alcohol. On those nights, I was immersed in mindless sleep, and free from the ongoing nightmare.

That dream haunted me for over twenty years. There was an episode which still sticks out. We are fleeing through a field where raw sewerage gurgles out of little springs. My family and I were running for our lives through this mess of gray water. I still don't know the meaning but now interpret it as all the shit in Phil's life starting to come to the surface. The nightmare dreams continued relentlessly until I was in my early forties.

Then one night there seemed to be a concluding episode. My family and I were walking through a gravel pit, a dry and lifeless place. The world was dying around us. We were on a worn dirt path through the pit when we came to a four-way intersection marked by large stones. Leaning against the rocks around the pit were dying people. I chose the path to the right, trying to avoid any contact with the near-dead around us. As we started off one of the poor souls said, "It's all uphill that way. There's nothing up that way. The walk out of here alone will kill you."

Somehow I knew differently and I dragged my family along that path. We got out of the gravel pit and into the woods. These woods were still healthy and had not been poisoned by the gathering death around us. We continued following a stream and drinking its sweet waters as we followed it uphill. There high up on the hill at the base of a huge mountain was a castle-like structure built into the cliffs. It was built to look as if it were part of the mountain rather than a structure. The sweet water we were drinking ran out of its base. The whole place looked like a pile of stone until we got up close. My family and I approached the structure and saw a big stone door, which was open. We went inside and the interior was enormous. Windows had somehow been crafted above the floors and all this light, even and strong, came down from above. It seemed to have a soft quality that was imperceptible at first because of its power. The brook with the sweet waters of life came out of a spring in the side of one of the rough walls. The world around us outside was dying, so we went inside and I instinctively closed and latched the massive door.

We learned to grow our own food and the spring not only gave us water but somehow sustained all our needs. From inside the castle we could look out and see the world die. Beyond the castle, the valley where our stream of life was running stayed green, and the trees, birds and other life forms that fed on the water did not die. The stream would end at the gravel pit where the flow ran dry. The water by then had blackened, poisoned by the death and destruction it encountered near the end of its route.

And with that the dream stopped, and I was left wondering for a long time why it just ended. What was the meaning of such an ending for a long running dream that was never to come back again? I also wondered how long we could really have lived there isolated from the world. Maybe the destruction was only in the area we could see? That perhaps just over the next hill life might be continuing on as normal for some people? The dream ended at a time when Phil's life seemed to be imploding.

For a while I was quite successful using the façade of this person Phil. At least the trauma of my youth seemed to be fading. That was a blessing in itself.

It was a tough act but I was good at it. I had built a tough rugged skin that no one could penetrate. To the world I was this tough rugged guy for that's all I would ever show. The tough exterior of Phil was all the world ever needed to see. But inside was Violet, scarred and running the controls feverishly, trying to save her life from detection and persecution.

I built Phil into a person who was respected. He appeared to have a good life with a wife and a son. Phil was a respected professional who had trained many men in the art of land surveying. It was where he made his living. I built Phil into a respected businessman of the community. But all the while it was some kind of tragic joke because really, Phil never existed. He never had a soul. He was a defense that I, Violet had put together to shield me from the world and all its hurt.

He had been my castle in the side of the mountain in which I lived while I watched the world suffer around me. But like the castle there was something wrong. For a while those around Phil flourished. Life seemed like it just could go on happily forever. In mathematical theory it might have been true but when you enter the human equation it is a pipe dream. For as humans we need more than food, water and air. We are social people and deep down we need to be with people. We can not lead a life living isolated in a fortress.

In time I could no longer stand the isolation of living within this shell I had created. Problems began to appear with the defenses. The shell had become so hard and heavy through the years that the weight grew to be too much. Deep ruts were being cut into my soul by the very weight of it.

The more successful I made Phil, the more miserable I became. I began to drink tremendous amounts of alcohol. With all the alcohol, weight gain became a constant battle. I was consuming at least 14 drinks a day after work. I was using drink to suppress things. But something was wrong, I knew I was trying to avoid something. Now those feelings of being pursued were coming to me during the day. The dream was turning into a reality. I was running scared from something I did not understand.

Back then I believed that if I tried hard enough that I could become Phil; that I could make it all work. I was in denial about what existed at my most innermost core. How I could I accept it? The world would never understand. So as I lived within Phil, I tried with all my heart and soul to be him. I really did. I tried and tried. It hurt every step of the way. If I really try at something and care about it, I never fail. Never! I always find a way. But here I tried all my life to be a boy and was failing miserably at it. Now I had become a man and the struggle became even harder.

To try to become Phil, I did ever more dangerous stuff as time went on. It was not so much that I had a death wish but more like I didn't care if I lived or died. I wasn't going to actively kill myself but if something happened it would have been okay. There is no one more dangerous than someone who has nothing to lose but a life of pain. And so I lived a life of danger. Winter hiking, fast cars, boats, snowmobiles, anything that I could take right to the brink of disaster, then back off just a bit and ride that dangerous edge. I would tempt fate and marvel as to what a man I was. But it was all as hollow as the person that I was presenting to the world. It was all so empty.

So my life became a continuing run of dangerous events. What is strange with life is that if you don't care if you live or die, there is some kind of power there that carries you through unharmed. By the sheer fact of not caring about dying, death just passes right by. It is only when you begin to care in life that you get hurt. I now recognize Phil's behavior as suicidal for eventually death would catch him. That all it had to do was stop just once, and the game for me would have been over. The thought intrigued me as to what my death would be. Would I fall overboard when by myself 30 miles out to sea? Maybe I'd end up setting the snowmobile wrong in a curve and, instead of brushing a tree, hitting it head-on? Or maybe I would break a leg on a winter hike above tree line when the wind chill was way below zero, when inactivity would guarantee death in a very short time. Maybe the tires on the sports car might not grab at the end of that four-wheel drift while sliding around that curve and maybe I would end up in the woods -- to die in the woods where life made sense. Maybe I would just end up passing out at the wheel while driving home from some bar, taking some innocent people with me. I began studying bridge abutments. I thought if I got the car above 100mph and just hit a bridge, that it would be over quickly. Just driving on the asphalt one moment and then careening through the stars in the sky the next – all the confusion, misery and the pain gone forever.

Through time I just got weak from the heaviness of the load. A person cannot live isolated forever in a castle and have any quality of life. The life of Violet was suffocating. Inside my armor I had everything I needed to survive. But the inner light of my soul was dimming as it never got refreshed by the healing light of the daytime. Violet would die if she stayed inside of that shell. If Violet died, so would Phil as he never really existed anyway.

Then one day it was as if worlds collided. I was on the couch hung over from the night before when suddenly everything snapped into place. It was like large turbines within me that were never used suddenly came to life. A pureness of thought came to me the likes of which I had never had before. If there was to be any survival at all it would have to be Violet.. Phil could not live without Violet but Violet could live without Phil. It was as easy as a mathematical equation. Why had it taken me so long to come to this conclusion as the answer was clearly black and white?

The tool I used all those years was denial. With denial I could cloud the equation to the point where it was obscured by a constantly whirling cloud. Keep the dust kicked up and you lose perspective for what's going on. When you're in denial, you don't know you're in denial. For if you knew you were in denial, then obviously you would not be in it. It is this closed loop that as time goes on gets faster and faster, and smaller in diameter until it turns into a torrent of destruction -- like a tornado of the mind. The only way to end it would be to stop the denial and end the loop. On that day the loop was broken. The denial was ended. Violet stopped working the controls of Phil. And like in the Wizard of Oz it was discovered that this formidable man called Phil was actually being run by a scared woman behind a curtain of deceit.

In that moment of time, there was bliss. The inner light shown out briefly and brightly. But soon the light was fighting to survive because after being tucked away for so long the light had grown weak. The winds of adversity blew so hard that the light of the candle would flicker. If I could have extinguished that light and have Phil survive I would have put that flame out in a heartbeat. But that flame was not the heartbeat of Phil; it was mine, and I could not kill myself without killing Phil. We were one total messed up package.

What came up next was the most heart wrenching part of my life. I could not just cast this shell off. I had to start dismantling it bit by bit -- one agonizing piece at a time -- just as I had assembled it, for it had been designed to last a lifetime. I was married at the time and this was a tragedy beyond belief for my wife. Our marriage was for the long run, and we had grown accustomed to living with each other. If I knew my life was going to turn out as such I never would have gotten married. But then my son would not have been born. He is a wonderful person and I miss his presence in my life. We never seem to talk. It still breaks my heart.

Through all of this I had to persevere. To thine own self be true. If I could not live a genuine life, then I could not live at all. I would not have survived trying to be Phil any longer. It was just not an option. There was no way out.

How I hurt at night listening to my wife weep in the other room. I destroyed her life right in front of my own tear-swollen eyes. But it was so primal. Violet had to be the survivor or no one would survive. The force of life knows nothing other than to continue -- it is so basic, so primitive, yet so strong. So survive I did.

No matter how things turned out after or how things were at the time, Phil's wife was loyal until the end. She told me she would stay and help out until I had surgery and then she would be gone. So for a while the misery that Phil suffered became hers too.

She stayed despite the comments from work, from friends and relatives always questioning why she was still there. But she was loyal to the end and stayed until after I had surgery. Then, when there was absolutely no chance of Phil returning, she left. I will always deeply regret how things turned out for her but I had no choice. It was tragic and it hurt like hell but I had to let her go.

So I started to take apart that castle at the base of the mountain. When the walls came down I was amazed that what I thought in my dream were windows with light from above, were actually windows to Violet's soul and that it was her purity and love presented in the only way she knew how that had kept everything together for so long.

It was only after I took care of my mother and our family; only after I raised my son; only after all my obligations were met except for the one which was supposed to be forever, that I finally let go of the artificial facade.

I had carried this load for too long, Daddy, and I have to set it down. If only you could reach out and touch me, to tell your daughter that you understand, and brush the tears from my eyes and tell me everything will be okay. To tell me you forgive me for killing Phil. There are many people who still miss him and cannot move on. But fate has seen to it that on this planet we were not meant to meet. I will never know your thoughts.

Chapter 8

Daddy, I want to tell you about the last time that I tried to be Phil and how it ended so terribly that the facade of Phil had to go. I had gone on a camping trip with my wife, Jack, Pete and his two sons. I had done some work for Pete and we had become friends. Sometimes Pete and his two sons would go stripper fishing in the mouth of the Merrimack River with Jack and me. And now we had planned a week-long fishing and camping trip.

The super cab was packed with gear. Inside were sleeping bags, blankets, and all the stuff necessary for a week of camping. The back of the truck had tents, coolers and the johnboat tied on top. Behind the truck the 22-foot Islander followed on its trailer. The truck and the boat were the ultimate toys for boys. The truck was a fully restored 1979 Ford Super cab. The truck had been hand built for me by the son of a good friend. Bob, the builder of the truck, had quoted me a price of $6,000 to restore it, and now the bill was up around $12,000 before it left his shop. And I'd still had to put in a few thousand more after that.

It was midnight black, inside and out, with a custom flat bed on the back. Even the bed was a work of art, with an oak plank deck, and the rest black tubular steel. The upper part of the bed behind the cab that faced backward was done with polished diamond plate complementing the blackness of the paint by its brilliant reflections. Complete with directional chrome mages and huge tires it was a beautiful sight to behold. Just the sheer size of it attracted people, let alone its dazzling beauty. It was a flatbed and without the cargo racks it was a joy to see.

It was old enough that many people were clueless as to what year it was. A few even asked if it was new. Why not? Everything on the truck looked brand new. Under the hood was just as magnificent as the exterior. It had a fully rebuilt 460 engine with an edlebrock high rise intake manifold topped with a huge four barrel Holley. Everything was chrome or midnight black.

Matched to the motor was the sweetest tuned dual exhaust. Just revving the motor was a thrill, let alone driving it. Bob had to custom mount the motor, because 4x4 Fords never came with 460s in 1979. The motor was actually too much for the drive train. Bob warned me not to beat on it too much as I would be able to snap an axle easily. That actually happened one night when I had a good buzz on and was coming home from bowling. I decided to horror show Ben who used to be a very close fishing companion but had grown distant the last few years. It was late and quiet as I went by his house. I stopped just beyond the house and lit up the tires, holding the truck back with the brake and putting out a huge smoke show. Went to the end of the block, and around the corner lighting them up again. Then I went down another few hundred feet to the corner of the main road, lighting the tires up one last time and wailing on it. The truck started to hop, and before I could back off there was an explosion that rang out in the quiet fall night air. The front differential had exploded and the drive shaft had augured into the asphalt. After that I was careful to never overpower the running gear.

By now I'd had the truck for about 4 years and it was still as sweet as when I first got it. Everything was packed. My pal Jack and I were on our way to Hermit Island in Maine. It was sort of an island, connected to shore by a strip of sand. This sand was never under water except every few years during really bad storms. The truck was running nice, the exhaust growling with each shift. We were following our other friend Pete and his 2 kids. They were in his beater station wagon. My wife was following us in her car, behind the boat.

The boat was a 22 foot aluminum Starcraft Islander with a Yamaha 175 hp outboard on the back. The boat was definitely driven by the motor. On a calm sea the boat was capable of 40+ mph, fast for a cabin cruiser. It had a wide deep V hull and a great fishing platform on the back. I had water-skied behind it off Plum Island one calm day.

Once we got off the freeway the trouble began. The truck started running rough. One of the problems that occurred occasionally was that one of the floats in the carburetor would stick and the truck would run rich. The quick fix was to remove this little cover on the side of the curb, an adjustment port that would drain the carb. It seemed to free up the float and it would go for a few months without sticking again. Well the damn carb was acting up again and the truck was running rich. Just what I needed, it only got six miles a gallon on a good day. The truck had two 20-gallon tanks and it would burn right through them. On a trip to Salisbury the truck would use 30 gallons of gas and the boat at 2 mpg would use at least 40 gallons, so an average trip was 70+ gallons.

Well I nursed the truck and boat down the road, pushing the clutch in and revving the motor to clear it when it was bogged. When there was enough room on the road I pulled over and did my little routine with the carb that set the truck to running right again. I was a little angry about getting gas on my hands. I wiped them on a rag, fired up the truck, fired up a joint and roared down the road towards Hermit Island.

About 10 miles before Hermit Island on the left is the public boat launch. We would come back to that tomorrow. For now we all went to the campground, made camp and started supper. Here was the start of my troubles, I did not have time to shop with Pete and that turned out to be a disaster. All summer I had been dieting and losing weight. I had eliminated all oils and ate very little meat. Well all Pete bought was basically meat and potatoes. There were eggs, onions and veggies for a beef stew and five different meals consisting of beef. And to cook it all, Pete had bought a big jug of Wesson oil. If I ever used oil it was just a drop of olive oil. To be staring at a half gallon of 30 weight was scary. First I would think you would never use that much heavyweight oil in your life, let alone in one week. So supper consisted of steak on the grill and potatoes fried in Wesson. We could not bake potatoes. Why? Because despite the $100 worth of meat, we had no tinfoil, no butter or margarine, just Wesson to cook with.

I made a comment to Pete about all the meat and he gruffly told me that it was a camping trip, and men ate meat while camping. Was that a put down? Seemed like it but I let it slide. My wife and I ate, then retired to our tent which was across the dirt road from Pete's site. Pete's site was really nice, at the edge of a tidal pond where tomorrow we would anchor the boat.

Getting up the next morning we had bacon, eggs, potatoes and onions fried in Wesson oil. By now my stomach was beginning to tie up in knots. With breakfast done it was shower time. I hated the community shower. I washed up quickly and went back to the camp. My wife, Jack and I got in the super cab, and Pete and the two boys went in the wagon and we towed the boat back to the public launch. The launch went out onto the Penobscot River. We splashed the boat and went upstream to Bath and the boatyards. It was a cool day for August, it looked like light rain might fall at any moment. Visibility was good, at least a mile. The Penobscot is an incredible river. The average depth seemed to be about 100 feet. No wonder the shipyard, which was about 15 miles upstream could turn out such huge ships. Last year when we all were on the river, the shipyard launched a huge ship. My boat looked like a little speck on the water next to that ship. The wake alone from this boat was about 6 feet. We had fun even though the weather was gray. We docked at the town pier, went uptown and ate. Afterwards, we all piled in the boat, gassed it up at a marina and set off for Hermit Island.

The trip down river was laid back, with the boat purring along at 28 mph. It was capable of at least 15 miles per hour more but 28 was the magic speed when the boat and the motor were in harmony. The shoreline rolled by with new sites and delights to see around every bend. Pete and his two boys were taking turns steering. I was watching the channel markers and the depth finder. Also I was putting way points into the GPS so I could navigate back upstream even in solid fog. Although Hermit Island was only 15 miles away by land, by sea it was 30+ miles. In time we cleared the river. At the mouth was an old fort. With some squinting and a little imagination, you could see the cannonade and smell the smoke. The river was narrow at that point and the fort well placed. Then we were on the sea and went right between some huge islands. It looked as if there was only one huge house on each island -- lifestyles of the rich and famous. We all talked about what it would be like to be rich enough to live there year round and let the rest of the world go on without us.

After clearing the islands, we had to go around a large peninsula, which meant about 15 miles of open ocean. The waves were around two-to-four feet, and we had to slow to just over 20 mph. The islander most of the time was a great boat, it towed well and had made many trips to Lake Ontario, along with hundreds of trips to Salisbury. It towed easily, the only drawback is that it is too light for any seas over four feet. But usually I checked the radio for the sea reports before going out and did not have much trouble.

One time however Jack and I went out 30 miles. It was dead calm and the seas were flat. We were out at the fishing grounds in 45 minutes. We hooked up the cod jigs and cast out. I got to jig my line twice when suddenly the wind started to blow. It went up to gale force in just a few minutes. I screamed to Jack, "reel it up!" Frantically I spun the handle on my reel. Got the Jig in the boat, threw the rod to the floor and went to the wheel. The wind was driving us with the waves, which in an instant had risen up three to six feet. The motor roared to life. In the trough of the next wave I spun the boat around and put the bow into the wind. I would have ridden the waves with the wind but the direction was out to sea. Being 30 miles out already, I had only about a 10 gallons safety margin on the fuel. If the wind blew us out 20 more miles there would not be enough gas to get back in.

The wind now was up to what seemed hurricane force. The waves now were eight to ten feet. It was insane! At the top of the wave the whole front half of the boat was in the air. Then the bow would drop with the intensity of a carnival ride. The stern of the boat would come right out of the water and I'd have to cut the throttle so as not to spin the prop off when it was out of the water. Then the boat would slide down the wave into the trough. The oncoming waves were practically straight up, steep and very close together. Once in the trough the bow would go into the wall of the next wave. The wall of water would bury the boat all the way to the cabin. Just when it seemed the boat would continue straight under the water and sink, the bow would pop up out of the water. Huge amounts of water were thrown back into the boat. Then the throttle had to go back to full open to climb up the wall of the wave. Both bilge pumps were on high and we were filling with water.

We were sinking. My mind was racing, as much as I did not want to go further out to sea the only way we were going to make it was to turn and go with the waves. It would be death defying turning now in the troughs. I was screaming at Jack so he could hear my plan when just as suddenly as it had started, the wind stopped. The waves started to subside but continued at about five to six feet for the rest of the day. It took almost six hours to return to shore --- a trip that normally took only 45 minutes. Jack and I took turns, alternating between steering and getting a face full of water with every wave, then taking a turn to duck down and drink rum and coke. Just mixing a drink was absurdly difficult, and in this situation just plain stupid, but we were determined to drink the booze.

Well nothing like that happened this trip. The seas were just average pain-in-the-ass rough and before long we were entering the long narrow bay to Hermits Island. When the water grew calmer, Pete and his boys went back to driving while Jack and I mixed rum and cokes. I longed to fire up a joint, but had been warned by Pete not to let his kids ever see that stuff.

At the final entrance to Hermit Island I took over the helm again. There was one tricky spot where the channel was only ten feet wide and you had to hit the spot just right or risk looking like a tourist when your motor grounded out on the mussel bed. We cleared the spot like old pros and continued up to the backwater where we could anchor about 200 feet away from Pete's campsite. His site was the best on the island. It was on the backside of the island, out of the wind, and it overlooked the backwater tidal pond where the boat was anchored.

We had supper, sat around the fire for a while, then my wife and I went across the dirt road to our tent and retired for the evening. The next day we were going out on the ocean to try and find some fish.

About noon the next day Jack and I rowed out in the johnboat to the Islander. The whole stern and motor was resting on the mud. If the wind was wrong when the tide went out, it would blow the stern of the boat, which instead of following the current would be blown aground. At low tide the spot where the boats were anchored was only about 30' wide.

We found that if we stood on the bow and shifted our weight up and down, the boat would inch forward toward the water, sliding downhill on the mud. So there we were doing some sort of crazy dance for the next 15 minutes until the boat was free. My wife left for home as she was only staying until Tuesday. The rest of us got on the boat and went out to sea to fish. We had absolutely no luck. During the boat trip we went across the bay from Hermits Island to another long bay and bought lobsters for supper.

On the way back to Hermit Island we went slow and stopped often, filling the coolers with seaweed. Jack and I were back on the daily rum-and-coke routine. I had cut my drinking about in half recently so I only had about eight drinks instead of my usual 16-18 a day from a year before. Back on the island we built a roaring fire, threw the seaweed on top, laid down a layer of lobsters, and then the rest of the seaweed on top of it all. The smell of the smoke was awful but the lobsters once cooked were awesome.

By now my stomach was wretched with nothing in it but meat, fried potatoes, and now lobster with old butter from the camp store. Jack was pretty much hammered and I told them I was going to lie down, as I didn't feel well, even though it was still daylight. I lay down in the tent, napping off and on while Jack and Pete drank and sat by the fire. I could hear them talking in muffled voices well into the night.

Jack had been made aware that I thought that I was suffering from Gender Identity Disorder and that I was taking steps to deal with it.

I had told him one day while we were out fishing. I told him I needed time to figure out what was going on in my life and that he needed to swear he would not tell anyone. He swore he would tell no one so I could have some time to figure things out. At that time I was Violet at home but Phil to all on the outside.

So little did I know that as they sat and talked in muffled tones by the fire that Jack was breaking his oath to me and telling Pete about Violet.

Later that night the wind was kicking up and I knew the tide was going out so I walked across the road to Pete's camp to look out on the boat. It was about 3am and the moon was out. I was going to row the john boat out and spend the rest of the night on the boat to keep it from grounding as the tide went out, but I could see the wind was not coming from a direction that would cause the boat to ground. Going back through Pete's camp, I stooped at the table and took a juice box from the cooler. We had all chipped in for it. I closed the cooler and was heading across the road back to my tent when the flap of Pete's tent flew open, he shined his flashlight on me and said "I never would have believed it"

"What" I replied.

"You know what I mean!" was his response. I was clueless about what it all meant and went back to bed. When I got up in the morning, Pete was packing up his gear. I crossed the dirt road and asked what was wrong. "We're leaving" was his response.

"MY son was sleeping there by the fire and you were on the other side of that rock watching him sleep and doing God knows what."

My brain hurt. What was he saying? I looked at the rock. It was at the edge of the tidal pool. The backside of where I was supposedly standing was in the mud and seaweed and would have showed footprints. He thought that I was standing behind that rock for hours, in the mud and seaweed spying on the camp on the off-chance that one of his sons couldn't sleep and would pull his sleeping bag out and sleep outside. And for what? To watch him sleep? The shore of the tidal pond was rugged and it would have been damn near impossible to stand there. Other than going through his campsite or through three feet of mud in the basin, there was no other way to this damned rock. What made him think that I had been there? I didn't get it. My brain was hurting, there was a hum beginning in my ears, and I was getting unstable on my feet. I didn't understand, I didn't get it. What was he saying?

"Besides" he said "I know about your issues. If your capable of that, you're capable of anything" Wham!!! Now I got it! Jack's hushed, drunken words around the fire last night were about my problems. I knew that my trust had been broken last night.

My head was swimming. I turned to Jack. "What do you have to say about this?" I asked. Jack, who had enjoyed being out on the ocean on my boat for these past eight years; Jack whom I treated like a brother; Jack who was at my office after hours five days out of seven a week drinking. Jack took a sip off his coffee, a drag of his cigarette and said "Well, you have been acting pretty strange lately!" The words and smoke were mixing together, poisoning the air.

I was losing my mind. "So you also think I'm a child molester?" I was gasping for air. I could not breathe. I would kill anyone I ever found hurting a child, for I was hurt as a child and carried a wound that would not heal. I had never told anyone. It was a deep wound in a dark place.

When I was 8, I went to work with the stepfather on an old mill building in Acton. It was an abandoned chair factory and they were draining the pond as the dam was weak and the new insurance would not cover it, if it should breach. I usually played alone. Up until this year when we moved I had always played with Jane. She had been my best friend. My exposure to boys was limited. Well, while playing around the millpond as it drained I met a couple of local boys. We poked in the mud and sand, which until a few hours ago had been underwater. The boys caught a large frog. "Watch this" said one as he took out a sharp jackknife. He made a quick shallow cut around the frog's neck and then using the knife and his thumb quickly pulled all the skin off the frog. The frog writhed with pain. I was horrified, sick to my stomach. He threw the frog on the sand where it wiggled and writhed, unable to do anything except shake with pain. In one swift motion, I stepped hard on the frog and ended its misery. The two boys thought I was joining in the fun and were jumping with excitement. Instead I was sick inside and deliberately ended the frog's torment. It had been a cruel lesson into the ways of boys.

As I stood there in front of Jack and Pete, I felt like that frog from 40 years ago. It felt as if those two friends had cut my heart out and threw it on the sand. I could see my heart writhing with pain in the dirt of the campfire. But unlike 40 years ago, there would be no act of mercy to end the pain. I was trapped, I couldn't breathe, and tears started to stream out my eyes. I ran to the tidal pond and threw the johnboat in the water. I had that incredible strength that comes with being out of control. I rowed to the boat, crying and gasping for air. I tied the johnboat off to the buoy, untied the Islander and started the motor. I was out of control. I flew down the backwaters full tilt, through no-wake zones and all, cleared the ten foot-wide channel at the end doing 25 mph with waves and wake flying everywhere. I didn't care if I lived or died. After about a half-hour of full out smashing on the waves I turned and went back at a safe speed. I didn't know what I was going to do but I was going to do something. Going back I went past a dock. A man jumped out of his chair on the dock and started a string of obscenities. Evidently he had gotten splashed on my first trip by. I just looked away and kept going. His curses fading in the distance.

When I got back to camp, Pete and his kids were gone. Jack was loading things into my truck. I went ballistic and started throwing his stuff out in the dirt. "If you can't be on my side when my whole world is coming undone you're no friend of mine. You broke your promise to me. As far as I'm concerned you can walk home." That would be the last words I said to a man who had been a close friend for 8 years. I threw my mountain bike in the back of my truck and took off. I drove to the end of the island where they made us park the boat trailer. The ground was irregular and it was frustrating trying to hookup the empty trailer. Tears poured down my face, and my long hair stuck to my wet cheeks. I lifted and heaved the trailer onto the ball, it seemed I had the strength of ten men. With the trailer finally hooked up, I took off for the launch some 15 miles away, stopping at the campsite on the way back through the island. I tore down my tent, stuffed it in the truck unrolled, sleeping bags, pillows, food, everything went in as one nasty lump, all heaved onto the truck. Next was the rest of the gear, dirty, wet, I didn't care -- stuff was just thrown into the truck in no logical order. It took about ten minutes to break camp.

Driving to the launch I finally stopped crying, I felt numb inside. I parked the boat and trailer, grabbed the mountain bike and headed back to the campground. I punished myself brutally on the ride back. At one time I could do 100 miles a day on my ten-speed. These were the worst 15 miles I ever rode.

When I got back to the campground, Jack and his gear were gone. I rode my bike to the empty campsite and looked around. I started sobbing again and went to the dock. I had already tied the johnboat to the truck when I broke camp. At the dock I borrowed a camp boat and rowed out to the islander. I started the motor on the islander and towed the rowboat back to the dock and exchanged the rowboat for my mountain bike. Then I headed away from Hermit Island forever. The sea was rough, I was full of grief. I deliberately went fast, slamming the boat into each wave with deliberate intensity. I hoped it would just break up and sink and that my pain and misery would end in the ocean. The pain would be over and it really wouldn't be my fault. But the boat just wouldn't break up, the damn thing held together despite the pounding it took. Rivets were breaking on the hull, things slammed, metal groaned. The bicycle bounced around the fishing platform, spray flying, tears flowing and, worst of all, a heart breaking, friendship and trust betrayed.

Finally I hit the river, full throttle all the way. The river and the world were a blur behind a cascade of tears. I reached the launch and trailored the boat for what would turn out to be the last time. I could see rivets missing in the hull. That boat was stronger than I ever believed. The drive home was torture, and I drove with tears staining my face the whole way. About half way home the truck started acting up again. Running rough, loading up with fuel. I kept pushing in the clutch and revving and clearing the motor. After what seemed like years the truck, bucking, banging and putting up smoke, turned up the road to my house. It was a ride from hell. I rounded the turn into the drive. The truck stalled, and I coasted to a stop. It was quiet. No more banging, rattling, no more load exhaust. It was quiet, and I sat there and sobbed. My wife, hearing the truck, came out and found me there on the seat of the truck. Between sobs I told her about Pete and Jack. She managed to coax me inside the house. I collapsed on the couch crying uncontrollably, I was out of control with grief. I couldn't stop crying. For three days I didn't move except for the bathroom. Food had no taste. I just could not stop crying. Something had to change.

The truck and boat sat where they stopped for a week. I was starting to have to make excuses to clients about why I had not parked the truck and boat in their usual place. After a week I fixed the carb on the truck and found that I needed a jump. The key was left in the run position when I pulled in from Maine. I jumped the truck. I turned the boat around and unhooked it in the part of the drive where the hose would reach and parked the truck. All the gear, the tent, the food, the stuff in the truck, the stuff on it, and the stuff in the boat sat there for 2 months. I hated them, the truck, the boat, Pete, Jack. I hated them all.

But most of all I hated myself. I had no control over my life anymore. Someone else was in control and the world hated her. I no longer wanted to be Phil. My life had always been such a mess.

After that I just gave up. The big black truck sat in the driveway mocking my 48 years of failure at trying to be a man. I had tried. God how I had tried and suffered in vain. I sought out one of my friends and explained to him how winter was coming on and my boat was parked partially blocking part of the driveway and I could not get inside of it because of the trauma. That I was starting to suffer from depression because of it. He made plans and came by the next weekend. We cleaned and washed the boat, finally washing the salt out of the motor. Next we emptied the back of the truck. What a mess, lots of stuff got thrown out, and I couldn't bear the smell, the stink of mold and death. I started the truck, the 460 boomed to life, and it seemed like the interior of the cab was filled with sadness as if it knew our time together was over. I parked and unhitched the boat, then parked the truck, the truck I had worshipped, and a boat I had loved. Whatever that was in me that made me crave such things was dead, I never got back inside either one of them again. Next year I sold them both, and put the money toward the deposit for a surgery that I hoped would end the pain.

Phil and I made arrangements for his surgery. Near his end he so wanted to be me that he took the final step towards transition. We sold everything he had -- boats, trucks, and snowmobiles -- every toy he had ever collected. We saved everything for the surgery.

By then what was left of Phil was suffering greatly as Violet began to emerge. I no longer could be there for Phil. For the first time in my life, I had to be there for me. So Daddy please forgive me for killing your son. It was greedy of me but I had to do it to survive.

Chapter 9

Well, Daddy, I underwent the surgery that Phil would not survive. So please let me tell you about my life, about the life of Violet Rose.

I woke up from surgery back in my hospital room, feeling sick from the anesthesia. I had been in surgery for more than six hours. I awoke to find myself throwing up in a stainless kidney pan that someone was holding under my chin. As I gained more awareness I could see a nurse standing on either side of the bed. It was coming back to me slowly and I thought back to just before surgery. Right when you are all prepped and the anesthesiologist is standing with the needle at the port on the IV the surgeon asks you one question "Yes or no? If you say no it's all right, we will stop immediately. But once you get this injection there is no stopping." I had something witty thing to say but my mouth was dry from fear, I was petrified, all I could do was nod my head yes. The needle went into the IV and that was it for Phil.

I was in Portland Oregon, the city of Roses. I was far from home and all alone. The operation had been gruesome. I knew it would be but in the two years of waiting for it, I had not allowed myself to dwell on the actual gore of it all. I was still not feeling any of the pain from surgery but I could tell my body was in shock. My mind was in a fog and my body was spent. My whole body had a slight tremor to it when I awoke. I had an IV in one arm hooked up to an automatic morphine dispenser. When it delivered a dose it would it made a low beep. It was already late afternoon and I spent the afternoon and that night napping off and on while the machine beeped. Each beep brought a feeling of reassurance that I was staying ahead of the pain. One of the nurses stayed for a few more hours. The morphine must have worked well as I drifted in and out of consciousness. I don't think that I had a cohesive thought until the next day.

The next day the morphine machine was turned off and instead a shot administered for the pain. As I lay in bed wasted from surgery, one of the nurses came in and declared, "Time to get up Violet, nothing is to be gained by staying in bed." She looked at me and continued, "We have to get the blood moving in your legs and you are going to take a shower."

"A shower! Are you kidding?" was all I could think. But she was serious. She pulled back the sheet, and I saw her do a double take. I was too weak to lift my head and look down. She continued on.

"Come on slide your legs over to the side of the bed and try to get up. Be a good girl."

I stirred and tried to move a little, but the pain was overwhelming. I gasped and laid my head back down.

"Violet you have to get up now." Her voice was stern this time, reminiscent of my mother trying to get me up for school.

In my blur of pain, all I could think, was "You bitch." I wanted to say, "I'd like to see you go through something like this." I really hated her at that moment, even though she was just trying to conscientiously do her job. This time I tried harder to move, and the pain was excruciating. I made it to the side of the bed, then my feet were on the floor. I would have kept heading to the floor had she not held me up. Firm hands guided me to the bathroom. A stainless steel rack holding an IV bag and a catheter bag was dragging behind me, making that agonizing journey with me. I got there one linoleum square at a time. I'd pick the center of the next square step and aim for it and with the ever-present hands of the nurse I made it. My body was shaking and my mind was just overloaded.

When we got into the bathroom the nurse took the robe off me. She had draped it on me as I got out of bed. There was a full-length mirror there in the bathroom in front of me. Thank God the nurse still had me as I almost passed out from the reflection. I was one big black bruise from just above my belly button down to the top of both knees. My stomach lurched with nausea. Then I saw the rest. My brain was on overload and trying to cope with the pain and not the image in the mirror. My genital area was completely taped off. A tube went up my urethra and out to the catheter. It came out through the tape and there were 3 other things that looked like little footballs dangling from lengths of tube.

The nurse went on, never missing a beat. "Violet you need to listen to me, you'll be expected to do this on your own after I show you."

God I tried to listen, even as the pain was numbing my brain. "Uh huh" was about the best I could manage.

She continued, "This one in the center is a drain for inside the vagina. You close this and empty the little football into the toilet like this."

I gagged as a clotted blood-like liquid dumped into the toilet. I wanted to puke, but managed to hold it back. I hurt so much I was afraid of what would happen if I became sick and started pulling muscles and stitches. The pain was just a white-hot knife, relentlessly stabbing me.

The nurse said, "This one is draining the left side of the vagina. And this one drains the right side of the vagina. They work the same as the other one." Then she had me drain them. Holding my shaking hands and making my fingers work for me.

"Good God, lady" I thought. "Give me a break" Even my brain hurt. If the nurse were to tell me at that moment that I wasn't going to make it I would have been happy to just lay down in bed and die, just to stop the pain.

But we were not done. Now it was the time to learn how to drain the catheter. "Turn this valve and disconnect the bag by pulling it out of the coupling." She dumped the bag into the toilet. Thank God she flushed the whole nasty mess away so I didn't have to stare down at it anymore. My stomach and my brain were spinning in opposite directions.

She positioned me in front of the toilet. I was little more then a claymation cartoon, a clay figure that is bent into a position and just stays there. To move at all hurt so I just stood there.

"Now Violet, you are going to have to try and teach yourself how to pee again. Can you be a good girl and try. She had the tube over the toilet. I tried and a pathetic little spurt came out.

"Good girl! Now I want you when you are awake and you feel like you have to pee to come in here and disconnect the bag and pee into the toilet. And also when you pee I want you to try practicing starting and stopping. And every 6 hours I want you to empty your fluid drains."

She looked me squarely in the face. "Do you understand?"

I was angry with her tone. It was like I had done something wrong. Looking back I see the wisdom in her actions as the patients after surgery could become totally dependent on them for care. The doctor and the staff wanted us to be independent and caring for ourselves as best we could.

So I tried to speak. I mumbled yes or something which she took as an affirmative. My aching body was longing for the bed but we were not done.

"OK Violet, time for a shower," the nurse said in a firm matronly manner.

"You've got to be kidding?" I mumbled. By now I was exhausted and could barely stand..

"No, I'm not kidding" was the uncompromising reply "You've got to learn how to take care of yourself and you have to start now."

Oh my God how I hated her at that moment. Didn't she know how much I hurt? With her help, I hobbled into the shower, one hand still hooked to the IV bag. With my left hand I feebly wiped soap onto a few parts of my body. She held me by my right arm while I slumped against the railing in the shower, hanging onto the handrail while the water ran down my hair and onto my bruised and shaking body. I didn't feel reborn at that moment. What had I done? Oh the pain.

She let me lean there for a while – just shaking, and leaning, and hanging on while the water washed over me. Then we were done. Oh thank God, please get me back to bed. She helped me dry. My beautiful hair was a knotted mess.

"Tomorrow I will help you wash your hair." She said. It seemed more like an order than an offer, but my hair was a terrible mess.

The catheter was hooked back up and I limped off to bed, the coat rack trailing behind, retracing the same squares back to the side of the bed. She got me back in bed and said "Now don't WE feel better"

My first thought was, "You probably fell better you Nazi bitch. But I hurt like hell." But, being a lady and knowing she was just doing what she had to do, I looked up and gave her a faint smile. She turned and left. My Nana taught me that if you can't say something good about someone, then don't say anything at all. Dad, at that moment I wanted to let loose a string of swears that would have made a sailor blush. But I just lay there. If I didn't move it didn't hurt as much

It was a fitful night. Every 6 hours a regular hospital nurse would come in and make sure I emptied my drains and assist me back to bed. I was starting to be overcome by the pain. I remember the words of my friend Kathy before I went into surgery "You make sure they give you enough pain killer. You have to stay ahead of the pain if you are going to heal."

Now I could see what she meant. At the time they were giving me a shot every 12 hours. But I could feel the pain building between shots, and it was beginning to overtake me.

True to her word the specialty nurse was back the next day. I told her how much I was beginning to hurt.

"Why didn't you say something sooner? Everybody's tolerance is different, so we started you at the lowest dose. Would you like us to increase it?" she asked.

"Please do!" I begged. "Give me the maximum. I hurt like hell…." By now my body had a visible tremor from the shock and the pain.

She went out and got a staff nurse and they gave me a shot. The specialty nurse hung around and chatted, making me drink water, getting me to relax while the pain subsided. She kept feeding me water and had a soft tone in her voice.

She checked to make sure I was using the little machine she gave me to do breathing exercises with and was happy that I was using it on schedule.

"We have to get you to keep up on your fluids as the IV is coming out soon"

Hey, now there was good news. Maybe things were looking up. By then the shot was working and the pain was getting smaller. Mmmm my brain was free of the pain for a moment.

Then she was at it again with that matronly tone, a tone I hate. "Let's go, let's wash your hair."

Daddy, at that moment I hated her, and hated that condescending tone of voice. I felt like a piece of spaghetti left in the water all night. If I could have lifted a hand I would have slapped the bitch. But she just kept right at me.

"Let's go. Get up." She ordered.

Daddy, did you ever get mad at any of your drill sergeants?

Once again, I slipped over the side of the bed and slowly and ever so painfully lowered myself to the floor. She draped a robe over me and I hobbled over to the bathroom, my coat rack apparatus dragging behind.

I went through the routine for her, emptying the fluid drains and hooking them back up; emptying the catheter and trying to pee. All the water she gave me had the proper effect. I was able to pee through the tube but I did not have the control to be able to stop and start again.

She was pleased anyway. "We have 8 more days before the catheter comes out. We need to retrain you to pee by then"

Boy that was a sobering thought. In nine more days I had to be on a plane to go home. Christ, I was a mess. I was running from immense pain, I didn't know how to pee. I've got some Nazi pushing me around the hospital room. I'll tell you, Daddy, I was becoming overwhelmed. What had I signed up for? This wasn't in the brochure.

Well Daddy, it was a hard time for a while. I kept the curtains closed. Every once in a while I looked outside. It was January in Portland and unseasonably cold. It had even snowed which is unusual for that area at that time of year. Outside the window were community gardens, all in a row – dead plants clinging to poles, all frozen in time by a fresh snow. How sad I thought at first. Everything is dead. Before I left I came to believe the picture outside was appropriate, because I too was in a winter of my life. That a fresh spring was just around the corner and that my new life would grow into something productive just like those gardens would come spring.

I lost track of time for a while. Shots for pain came every six hours. So when the shots took hold I would follow the squares to the bathroom, fourteen squares going over and fourteen back. Was it 12 noon or midnight? Was it 6am or 6pm? The clock must have been broken. After a shot, the hands on the clock would whirl around for a few hours. Then as it came time for my next shot, the clock would slow down. Then I could hear every second tick by. What was wrong with that clock? I figured they must have been giving the clock shots also. My mind was a dull blob. Periodically food would show up. I'd wake up and it would be on a tray next to me. I'd push it around with my fork and eat a few bites. How could they cook food with no flavor? It didn't matter if I ate; they were still feeding me with an IV. After a few bites sleep would return and the next time I awoke, the food would be gone.

Daddy, on the third day a whole new source of misery came to call. I had to stop taking hormones 2 weeks before surgery. Now, post-surgery my body had no hormones at all and no way to produce them. I went into full-blown menopause. I was hot, I was cold. I was hot and cold at the same time. And all the while I was still shaking from the shock of surgery. In short, I was a mess. It's a wonder I did not wear out the room's heating and cooling unit the way I turned up the heat, then the cold, full blast.

Daddy, it was near impossible to sleep. I had the nurses bring me a clean set of sheets before I tried to sleep for the night. I would fall asleep shivering under a sheet. An hour later I would wake up sweating to death, soaked and wringing wet. I would get up and change the sheet and my Johnny. By the time I got back into bed I was shivering again and would get back under the sheet and shiver and shake myself back to sleep. An hour later I would be a puddle of sweat again. It went on for days. For a while I was wondering if I was healing at all. Every trip to the bathroom hurt as much as the last one.

On the sixth day I was allowed to start taking the hormones and, thank God, the menopause stopped. All the while I was still doing my daily routines and was quite proud of myself. I could pee in the toilet, and stop and go when I wanted. I felt like some young girl who just learned to use the toilet. I wanted to tell my Mommy. But, Mommy you were not there. The only one I had to talk to was the watchful nurse who kept coming everyday.

In the past few days, her manner had softened a little. Until the sixth day came, then there was that tone in her voice again. Oh, how I hated it. Demanding and I thought, unfeeling. She was at it again.

"It's time to un-bandage your vagina and remove the packing" She said it so coldly like she was about to open some parcel of freight.

Off came the bandages, and, wow there was a lot of them. Then she started to remove "the packing." She started pulling out this incredibly long piece of gauze. It gave me the strangest feeling as she pulled it out and the air went in. The gauze was soaked bright red with blood, and I was beginning to feel nauseous. Then it was all out. I looked away before I got sick.

The nurse then unrolled some things all wrapped together in a towel. Inside were some things she called stints.

"These are your lifelong buddies now. Get used to them." She said breezily.

Inside were five stints as she called them, about 9 inches long, and they looked like clear plastic penises of different diameters.

"You have to dilate to keep the vagina from collapsing while it heals", she said in the same tone.

My mind was reeling. I knew I would have to do this to heal. What I wasn't prepared for was the flashback horror to when I was raped.

My breathing was getting very irregular. The nurse was getting more insistent.

"We've got to do this." She said sternly.

"Stick it up your own crotch" my mind wanted to shout. But I didn't dare say it to the Nazi nurse. So I tried. Oh Daddy, it hurt so much. She lubricated the smallest stint and helped me insert it into the vagina. Oh, Daddy the pain. It was like sticking a broom handle in a knife wound. I was panting from the pain and the flashback. I could barely breathe. Then it was in. Then another lesson.

" Move it around and move it in and out past that tough spot." She said

"Are you kidding me!" The pain was so much that I didn't know if I was saying it or just thinking it. But she continued on with her firm manner until we were done. I pulled out the stint and fell back exhausted.

"Okay, Violet, get up. I need to show you how to douche and care for your equipment"

Now I had a formula to remember. So many ounces of soap go into the douche. Fill it with water of just the right temperature to this line, insert it and squeeze slowly. Really slowly at first. I quickly found the comfort band for the temperature of the water was very narrow.

"Now, Violet, you must do this four times a day for the first three weeks." I wasn't shocked because I had done some research prior to surgery, but still it was a daunting thought now that the reality was here.

"Then after three weeks, you can go to three times a day for two more weeks, then twice a day for two weeks and then once a day after that. And after a month you should be up to this size." She held up a stint that brought fear to my heart. At the time it looked like a telephone pole. She got me back to bed and left.

About two hours later my counselor from back home called. She asked how I was doing. Her call was all too convenient. I asked her if the Nazi nurse had called her.

She said " Why no. Is there a problem?" she was playing Mickey the Dunce to a tee.

I knew she would not tell me but I asked her so she would know that I knew what was going on. She had helped me along this far and knew my very soul. But I also knew hers by having spent so much time with her.

So I told her about how I had a panic attack and that I was dealing with it and would be much better the next time. The next time was only a couple of hours away, every four hours during the day for the next three weeks. Oh man, it seemed a painful sentence. But I promised her I would try. And I did.

After 10 days I left the hospital and flew to a friend's place in Florida. She was a close friend who had lent me support over the years. I was there for her when she was distraught over the fact that someone she truly loved had walked out the door as if the relationship didn't exist. So my friend moved away to Florida, away from the daily reminders of a broken heart in order to heal. She took me into her house and cared for me as lovingly as she would have cared for her sister. And we have been sisters since. I try to visit her as often as the time and the distance will allow. She is very dear to me.

When I got to Kathy's place, I was a mess. When I got up earlier that morning I took two percocet painkillers. When I got to airport I took two more. Even ten days later I still hurt like hell. So I took two more percs before the connecting flight. Carrying a catheter had its advantages when traveling -- I just would fall into a seat and never have to get up. The day before they tried to remove the catheter, but could not because I still had excessive swelling. They had taken the catheter out and I could not pee. After a few hours I was in complete agony. It was hard to believe that with all that pain, something new could be more painful. One of the male nurses came in and reinstalled the catheter. The relief was instantaneous; I rolled my head toward the nurse and said "Thank's hon that was better than sex." He just sat there and blushed.

So by the time Kathy found me at the airport I was pretty much back in claymation mode again. She took me home. Her daughters came by to welcome me. They sat me at the table. I took a sip off someone's drink and the next thing I knew it was morning. They had tucked me safely away in bed.

I am forever appreciative of, and indebted to Kathy's loving care. There was constant washing and bleaching of bloody sheets, towels and nightgowns -- I went through at least six towels a day. They had to be clean and sanitary, and this entailed a lot of work on her part. Her compassion never once flagged under all that heavy labor, and there was never a moment when I did I not feel surrounded by love and in the care of the kindest, most capable hands.

Over time the surgery healed and I was well again, off on a new life. I'm single now, Daddy. My life has been very challenging but I have continued to heal.

Now in order to heal completely, Daddy, I have to ask you this. "Can you forgive me for killing your son? Many people in the world are angry at me for killing Phil. Are you one of them?"

Daddy, near the end Phil knew he had to go. We knew that the two of us could not survive in the same body. If we both stayed then we would both die. There was no option. One of us had to go. Phil knew we would be happier if I survived. His life had been a mess up until that point.

I have tried to take myself and the best of what Phil had to offer and forge them into one person – sort of a metallurgic trick. You take two metals with different qualities and forge them together to form an alloy which is stronger and better than the two individual metals on their own. So now Phil and I have been forged into one person, who is much better than either one of us was alone. The heat of transition smelted us together for eternity. Part of Phil lives on inside of me forever, and to him I will always be grateful. At the end he knew it was the only way, and it was so brave of him. He must have got it from you, Daddy. For all the times I was there in the past for him, he gave his life so that I could continue to live. At the end he was there for me. Just as Rose in Titanic had to release the hand of her companion to live, your Violet Rose had to let go of her lifelong companion, your son, in order to survive.

Daddy, can you forgive me for killing your son? In reality he gave his life so that I might live. For awhile Violet Rose floated on her tiny raft of hope on the cold and turbulent seas of Phil's past life, all the while hoping for acceptance and a new life. I have to stop and cry for a while, Daddy. I'll try to not cry too loud so I can hear you in case you answer. But please wait for just awhile longer. I want to try and gather a little composure before I tell you a little more about your daughter Violet Rose.

Chapter 10

Well Daddy, it's been a long hard road to get here. I have wanted to be a woman all my life from as far back as I can remember. I used to have dreams that someone would kidnap me and take me to this weird place and turn me into a girl. I remember the dream was so exciting. I was always so elated when I had that dream, and when I woke up the memory would still be fresh. Did it work? Was I a girl? The dreams were so vivid I had to be a girl. I always had to check. Ugh, I'm still a boy! The feeling of elation went away quickly. The dream would come very frequently and each morning I would check and every morning the results were the same.

Now Daddy, every morning I wake up I still have to check and see. Oh thank God, I'm still a woman. It is wonderful! It is me! I have been set free to fly.

Daddy, a couple of weeks ago I was in Cocoa Beach at the condo I rented for the winter. I was upstairs trying to organize some of my thoughts to say to you. Curves –the fitness place for women where I usually work out --- was closed. I wanted to get in the exercise zone to think, and figured I'd go swimming. I was at the computer and looked up to see it raining. Drat. Being determined I went downstairs anyway. I got to the pool where raindrops were making small circles in the water. I put down the towel and my sunglasses on a covered table -- I had gotten into the habit of always taking sunglasses everywhere in Florida. Even though it is winter the sun is still blinding when it is out.

I began swimming in the pool. If I couldn't go to Curves then I was determined to swim 100 laps instead of my usual 60 -- a lap being one length of the pool. So Daddy, the strangest thing happened. It started to pour huge raindrops. The sky had opened up and a tropical downburst fell from the sky. The raindrops were so quick that you could not even see them. When they hit the surface, the pool water would send up this little blob of water, which would linger for a second. I laughed while swimming because somehow the pool looked like it had this really bad case of quivering goose bumps. The cloudburst went on for a while and stopped. And then moments later the sun was out. Florida is like that, Daddy. You might know that as all the pictures of you were on ships somewhere with your shirt off, so you had to be in warm places.

When I had finished my laps I went to the deep end of the pool and started treading water to relax my muscles from the laps. I bobbed about there, slowly moving my arms to stay afloat, just thinking about things. I stayed there treading water wondering if I had the courage to come see you. For I could not go to you without forgiving you because I did not want to visit you as an angry daughter and leave a bad impression. The first impression is so important.

So all of this was swimming through my brain while me body was swimming in the pool when for some reason my shadow had caught my eye. If I kept my legs together and just moved my arms the shadow in the bottom of the pool was like a dragonfly. My moving arms and the refraction of the water made the shadow of my arms look like delicate wings. All of a sudden it was I with the goose bumps. For then I knew I had my answer. At that point I could feel my heart fill with love for you. At that point I forgave you. At that point I knew I would have the courage to go through the gate to find out where you are, and to tell you that it was wrong of me to hate you. I was ready to leave the waters of sorrow and fly, to become your Dragonfly Daughter. I had begun life in the waters of the male world only to finally emerge and learn to soar.

So Daddy, I want to tell you I forgive you. We all lost. You never met your son and you lost your family. We all lost you. Paradise Lost. It was just the type of thing life does – it's nobody's fault. But I was a child and I needed something or someone to blame, and it was just easy to blame you. It was easier for me to deal with it that way. I'm sorry. Forgive me. I know that if you could have, you would have come back to Mom and me. That it was not your fault. But my life was such a mess that I needed a place to hang my pain, and that hook was you.

But Daddy, my life is getting so much better. I have stopped here to visit you on my way home from Florida. I rented a condo there for the winter. I don't know if you know what a condo is – it's sort of an apartment that you own. Well I rented this place to get out of the New England winters. You must remember them. My knees are arthritic and can no longer take the cold. So I went to Florida to heal. I had been working outside in October in the rain for almost 2 weeks last fall and my knees were very bad when I left for the south.

I have found Florida a place to heal. At first, I started gimping up and down the beach because I had put on extra weight over the summer since my weak knees prevented me from exercising. So now I was plodding as best I could down the beach. By the time I'd get back to the condo, I was worn out. I kept going day after day. I went a little further and a little faster each day. The sand was perfect for barefoot walking. It allowed me to take perfect steps with even pressure. There was no jarring on the knees from hard surfaces. To my amazement the knees started getting better. I could walk longer and longer, pretty soon I was walking four miles a day and feeling great. Walking along the shoreline was very invigorating. When the waves crash, the air is ionized, and it energizes those who breathe it. That is why there is always that clean crisp feel to ocean air. You were a sailor, so you must have loved the smell of the ocean air.

Well the strangest thing started happening. The better my body got, the better my mind was feeling. Being away from New England had given me the distance to gain a new perspective on my life. Not having to see images of a failed life refreshed me. I could go day-to-day just living in the now without constant reminders of the tragedy of the past. Also being away from people who knew my past also set my spirit to flying higher. There were never any slip-ups when people addressed me. I was always she. There was no one I ever had to feel sorry for because I had hurt them when I killed Phil. I was happy in the sunshine out behind the condo at the beach. Dad, I fished there a lot. The first two weeks in Florida, I spent walking the beach. I would stop and talk to the fishermen. First to see what they were catching, and secondly and most important to see what they were using.

They were all going for one type of fish – a pompano. It had no scales and its skin flashed in the bright Florida sunshine when out of the water. They are bright silver with just a little bit of shinny yellow on its bottom. It was a beautiful fish, pumpkin-seed shaped like a lot of the southern fish. At the same time it also looked like a mini tuna, with small mouths that pout. It was almost sad to see them bobby around in the pails of the fisherman. They looked so sad with their pouting faces. But such is the life of fish. Dad, did you ever feel sorry for the fish you caught? I do. Whenever I catch a fish and I am going to keep the fish and eat it, I apologize to the fish for its life is gone. It will no longer be swimming in the waters of life but has now become part of the food chain.

I am grateful daily for being at the top of the food chain. Imagine if something larger than us was to swoop down out of the sky and snatch us up for dinner. Well I convinced myself that it would be okay if I apologized first to the fish. Yeah, right! I'm sure it would never be right for the fish. So that is why I have a reverence for the spirit of the fish that is about to be released from its body.

So after two weeks of walking the beach, I went to the store and bought the same rod and tackle that I saw the fishermen on the beach using who caught the most fish. Dad, I'm not an engineer by accident, it's just me. There's a problem, you analyze the problem and come up with a solution. My solution worked very well. The first day I went fishing, I caught two nice sized Pompano.

I had met my next-door neighbors and we were becoming friends. So with the Pompano and their pouting mouths in my fish bucket I rushed upstairs to show them off. My neighbor Mary and I cleaned the fish. I told them they could have one. Her husband John was delighted. Mary suggested that we fix the fish for supper.

We sat on their deck. It was next to my condo, and we watched a magnificent sunset of gold and coral turn to purples and then to gray. That gentle Florida breeze and the distance kept the evil of my world away. The Pompano were cooking slowly on the electric grill behind us. Surely this had to be heaven.

We went inside and ate the fish. It was so good. I still love cod and haddock like the fish your father used to catch but this pompano was wonderful in its own way. I was instantly hooked on them, and I fished a lot.

I had my favorite spot, Dad. I would set up the chair, set the sand spike, bait the hooks and cast as far out as I could. The rod was placed in the sand spike, and I would sit and watch. There is so much life at the ocean to see that it always entertained me even if I caught no fish

The life at La Playa would start below the sand and get more magnificent as you went up. John had told me how to catch sand fleas for bait. They were strange things – sort of like a crab. I took this basket thing on a handle designed to catch them. It was made of galvanized mesh so the water would run out. At half tide or lower you could reach a drop off in the sand. If you pulled this basket up the edge of the sand it would come up half full of sand and shells. And mixed in with all of this were the sand fleas. They were comical little crustaceans with at least six legs. They had a hump-backed shell and if you picked them up they would draw their legs in tight. The big ones were about the size of an aggie marble and the small ones were about the size of a sunflower seed.

I made friends with a lot of seagulls that afternoon. Whenever I dumped a basket on the beach they would cluster around and watch. Once and a while one of them would put its head back to utter an impatient squawk. But mostly they watched and waited, and were patient while I poked in the pile for sand fleas. All I had to do was push around the piles and the sand fleas would run toward the ocean as fast as their little legs would carry them. Maybe they were really called sand "flees!" I would pick up the ones large enough for bait. Then I would go back to the water and the gulls had what they were waiting for. They would swoop in and eat the stragglers and pick through the pile for any that might be hiding. All the time the gulls were fighting and squawking amongst themselves.

I caught my first two Pompano that day. But I never used sand fleas again. I felt sorry for them. When I had to put them on the hook I had to stick the hook up through them, and their little legs would kick in pain. I felt terrible; they were way more developed than a dumb old worm or something like that. From then on I fished with frozen clams from Wal-mart. At least they were stupid clams and someone else had already killed them. After that, I never had the flock of gulls picking over the sand fleas. I had just one gull, an old and crafty one. Whenever

I went out, he was there. So when I fished I would throw him a piece of clam. He was good at eating it really quick before any other gulls could see him and come over to fight for the prize.

And that's how my days were spent at La Playa. Watching the end of the fishing rod and watching everything else around me. There were these tiny silly little birds which when the wave would recede they would run down with the receding water pecking at the sand. And when the next surge of water came back, they would race toward shore just ahead of the waves as fast as their little legs could carry them. They were relentless -- what a silly life.

There were other birds that did the same thing but they were a little larger and had Wilt Chamberlain legs. They walked around like little brothers. They had their strut and moves and they didn't care if their feet got a little wet. They were just eating and acting cool.

There were several kinds of seagulls. The ones like my fishing buddy are the same gulls as back home. Then there was this pack of these other gulls. I never could figure out what their act was all about. The only time I ever saw them was when I walked the beach. They were smaller than the other gulls and had orange bills. They hung around in these tight little packs at the water's edge all looking in the same direction like they were constantly waiting for something to happen.

When I walked the beach they would begrudgingly back away from the water as a group, all of them turned my way and watched me while I walked. They always looked like they had an attitude and wanted to say "Hey, we let you get away with it this time, don't let it happen again." And after I passed by they were back to the water's edge just waiting and watching.

Sitting and fishing with my buddy the gull, we saw many things. One day my fishing gull did not show up. I set up my gear and baited my hook, put the rod in the spike and turned to go back to the chair.

There standing next to my chair was this beat up old blue heron, a real old timer. He was missing a few feathers on his body from an old conflict or maybe just from old age. I stopped and looked at him. He was looking at me. I did not want him to fly away so I just stood there and we stared at each other. Then as I moved towards the chair he would back up. When I sat down he moved closer and was about 5 feet behind me just standing. People were walking by and taking pictures. It was kind of remarkable. He kept staring at the fish bucket. It had water in it but no fish, but I don't think he knew that.

So for the next two hours we engaged in this little dance. When I would walk down to the rod and reeled in the line to check the bait, he would walk down and stick his beak in the fish bucket looking for a snack. He was quite coy about it. It was like a game of red light when I was a kid. I would start to walk toward the rod, stop and turn around. He would be motionless staring at me as if I wouldn't notice that he was closer to the bucket.

I'd get down to the ocean ready to cast and glance back, and there that old heron would be standing by the fish bucket looking at me. I would have to turn and cast, reel in the slack and put the rod in the spike. When I would turn around the heron was still standing at the bucket supposedly in the same position but I could see water dripping off his beak.

I kept telling him "You're not fooling me. I know what you're up to." But he just kept standing there like some droopy-shouldered mischievous child. I could almost hear him saying "Hey, I didn't do nothing'"

After a while the heron got bored. He did not like the clams I threw him nor the crust of a sandwich. He wanted fish and for some reason I could not catch a single fish that day. The heron left and the fishing gull was immediately back. He must have been watching and biding his time. He came back and quietly ate up the pieces of clams and the crust of bread. He was good at keeping his prizes from the other gulls. So for the moment the fishing gull was content and quiet. We looked out at the blue green sea. That day we saw a dolphin -- a quick glimpse as it broke the surface. A little further out the pelicans were fishing. What a strange and wonderful bird. When they are on land they almost look ridiculous with their long beaks and necks tucked against them and defiant looking eyes starring back at you.

The pelicans in flight were pure beauty. They flew in groups of four to eight, and sometimes would soar along the shore way up high, barely having to move their wings in the constant ocean breezes, like a row of fighter pilots wing tip to wing tip in tight formation. Other times they would fly in a smaller group in staggered formation just barely over the waves with their wings almost touching the water. Sometimes as the wave would curl there would be a group of them sailing along just in front of the breaking wave. Maybe they were trying to show the surfers how it was done.

Today the pelicans were fishing. The fishing gull and I sat and watched them. The pelicans would fly along about 20 feet in the air. When they saw a fish they would tuck their wings back and fall from the sky, plummeting to the sea. Just before they hit the water, they would extend their necks and pull their wings tight to their bodies and crash into the sea, leaving an explosion of water where they hit. The fishing gull and I watched the pelicans and just lolled the afternoon away. There were no fish that day but the ocean nourished us in other ways.

I swear the fishing gull would follow me around when I was outside. One day it was just superb all day -- puffy clouds, light winds, the sound of the surf -- and I spent an extra long time walking the beach. This lone seagull swooped down at me. It was like a bombing run and then plop, he left a nasty white mess on my bare shoulder. I knew it was that damn fishing gull and that he was mad because we were not fishing. I chased him down the beach. He was a smart one, he joined a group of gulls and I could not pick him out.

I waded into the sea and washed my bare shoulder, and just for spite spent the day walking instead of fishing.

And so I spent many days walking and fishing the beach, observing and interacting with the life around me. My body and mind were healing in unison. And what was more important was that I was able to write again. Before I finally accepted myself I could not write. I used to write as a child but my life was hard and what I wrote was too dark so I stopped.

Then one day several years ago something happened. It was like lightening hit me. I felt totally alive for the first time in a long long while. I knew what I had to do. There was something I had to say. To write and write and write, so I could take the time to craft what I had to say, to be able to explain myself without fumbling for words. For in an instant I had found the strength to accept myself for who I am.

I had to write to my wife and son and explain myself. It was one of the hardest things I ever wrote. It took me two weeks working every night to come up with just 3 pages. How could I tell it all in just three tear-stained pages? For me, this was redemption, because once I admitted to myself who I was, all the things that I had stuffed in that dark place were allowed to come out. They came out with a rush, as if all the floodgates to an overflowing dam opened at once and drained the water from behind the dam. All that enormous pressure had been taken off the dam. And the dam although still strong was able for once in its life and just say "AHH"

So much did my soul feel relieved that I truly felt I had been born again at that moment. Needless to say my wife and son were not as thrilled with me. I was trying. I cut way back on my drinking and was feeling much better about myself. I started attending self-help groups and my wife went along trying to understand things. My spirits began to sag again as it seemed the whole world was against me. The life of a T is a constant battle for acceptance, and being an unwanted child, it was something I was never good at. I fell back in the bottle almost as bad as I was before, but I still held onto who I was. My appearance started changing. My hair was long and beautiful, nails long and clear coated. I could be taken for male or female. I was in an androgynous state -- a chrysalis. Then it happened. It was something that would change my life. I was driving and the blue lights came on behind me. I could feel the pain as the blue shaft of light cut through the car. I had been drinking heavily again and now there would be hell to pay.

I was arrested and put in jail for the night. Now I was a criminal. I spent the night on a hard bench watching the jail ants come and go out of a crack in the floor. I wondered what they were in here for -- stealing picnics or something worse?

So there I was the next day in front of the judge. I stood there, part he, part she, with a big knot of messy hair. The judge's words: "Trial in 2 weeks." It was two weeks of shameful hell. Then the trial, I tried to dodge the book but it hit me square, with one year's probation along with random drug and alcohol testing; and twenty-one weeks of mandatory alcohol awareness classes and mandatory AA. If I screwed up, the judge assured me he would send me to jail and I had no reason not to believe him.

I sobered up and walked the line. Near the end of the probation I started to write again. So the first thing I wrote was a letter to a friend in a support group who had been helping me along. She was to a T girl; she is no longer with us. Her name is Debbie. If you see her over there I'm sure she will tell you her story. I met Debbie a few years earlier when I was looking for a support group.

I went to the western part of the state. I was afraid and did not want to see anyone I knew. First I had to be interviewed in order to join the group. I met two representatives at a Bickford's restaurant. We talked for some time and then in telling my past I mentioned the town of Littleton. One of the girls perked up at the name. We talked and I found out she grew up in Littleton. We had never met or known about each other.

How odd life can be and what games it likes to play with me. I drove two hours to seek help away from my own local area, and end up having a hometown girl be one of the interviewers at the end of the trip. Her role was to be the one there to help me the most. It was just one of those unexplained ironies of life. After the alcoholic haze began to clear I sent her this letter to show that I eventually learned what she was trying to teach me. She had often times offered to go to AA with me knowing I had a problem. Dad I will read you the letter I wrote her.

Dear Debbie,

I was sentenced to 21 weeks of alcohol awareness classes, once a week on Wednesday nights in West Concord. I went there as Violet, and that caused quite a stir with the system. They did not know how to deal with me and started giving me individual sessions. But after one session I was frantic because the person who I met with started asking all kinds of personal questions. Questions like which bathroom I use, and whether I dressed as a woman when I have sex with my wife. When she found out that we did not have sex, as I don't see myself as a man climbing on top of a woman, she asked if I thought that I could have a rewarding marriage without having sex. Every question she asked for two hours was based on sex and the T issues in my life, even though I was there for drinking and driving, not some T related crime. This initial session was to evaluate me and see if she was going to put me in the men's or woman's group. How could I ever be open and honest in a men's group? After the first session she informed me that she was going on a four-week vacation and that I would have to have individual sessions until she came back. And when she came back she would then ask the women in the group if they minded if I joined their group. I told her that outside of work I lived entirely as a woman and there was absolutely no chance of me going in the men's group and that she would have to put me in the woman's group. The session ended and I stormed out of the room.

The following week my session was with the director of the program. The week leading up to that was very tough as I started having severe depression and self-doubts. But also there was an anger building within me as to why I should be treated like a second-class citizen. I wrote down all of my thoughts to present to the director and during the week sought out a T friend who is part of the second offenders program in eastern Massachusetts, and deals with the T part of the program. She was very upset with the things I had told her and immediately took it up with her superior. I went to the second meeting armed for battle and just laid it all on the director. Why should I get individual sessions when the court ordered group therapy? Why should I have had to answer such personal questions? Why did they feel that they had to identify the issues in my life and dwell on them while I was trying to deal with these issues? And then ask the group if they could accept me? If they could accept me? Why was my psychological health secondary to the group? I said all this without knowing about the fact that my friend's superior, who worked for the state, had called that morning and gave them holy hell. They were supposed to be sending someone to seminars about T issues and had not been doing so. He told them that if the problems were not dealt with that he would see to it that they lost their state funding. And he said that when the person who the week before had grilled me came back from her vacation, that he personally wanted to see her. With all of this going on, the director of the program told me next week to come to the women's session and that they were sorry about the treatment I had received up until now. When the person who went on vacation returned she was so upset at the turn of events that she quit. Good enough, she was a witch and should be more sensitive to the issues in the lives of people in the program. If I had not been such a strong person and had not gotten so angry over these things, and if I had not had an influential friend in the state, they would have walked all over me and not cared about my psychological well-being.

The sessions were boring and seemed to last forever but went without a hitch, and when I left, the entire group of woman was accepting. They had instantly taken to me when I told them about the psychologist who was on vacation and my treatment at her hands. And when she came back from vacation and quit, it seemed like the scene right out of the Wizard of Oz when Dorothy's house fell on the witch. Not a single woman there had a good thing to say about her. This woman had been running the group and all the girls hated her, and this outcome turned out to be good therapy for us all. Now the director was running the meetings, and we were all more at ease with her and we all talked about what some of the issues in our lives that drove us to drink. They were very interested in the T issues and learned about a few of the problems faced by us that they never had thought about. Good ground had been covered since I had been the first T they had to deal with, and I left feeling that maybe I made it easier for the next one.

Debbie, I have not drunk or smoked pot in over 8 months. It took me four AA sessions to even admit to myself that I was an alcoholic and a drug addict, another two to tell it to the group. Now that I have been clean for a while I can see clearer that even though I was trying to deal with the issues in my life, I had still been hiding in a bottle. I should have taken you up on your offer two years ago when you wanted to take me to an AA meeting, but at the time I was in denial and nothing you could have said would have made me go. However I am very grateful to you for caring enough to make the attempt.

Things now are going kind of good, and my wife is trying to be as accepting as possible. It is all very scary to us as things progress. Next month I start on hormones as the next step in my journey towards womanhood. We are both afraid of our jobs, making a living, dealing with friends and relatives, all of the stuff that goes along with being T.

I am very appreciative of you and the support you and the group gave to us. My wife also said you wrote her a while ago and asked if everything was ok. It was during a time when things were not and I apologize for not getting back to you. I miss you and the group and am looking forward to coming back and seeing you all in a few weeks. I am sorry for writing such a long letter but a lot has gone on. I have only touched on a few things but wanted to give you a good update. It is my fault that we have grown distant and not the fault of you or the group.

With lots of love
Violet Rose

Well Dad, I never saw her or the group again. If you see her, tell her thanks. She was one of the most influential people in helping me understand. But I'm sure she already knows.

Chapter 11

Well Daddy, it's starting to get late and I need to finish so I can go on with my journey back to my native New England, back to the beloved woods I think I know. I will not tell you much about transition. For it was like a tale of two cities. It was the best of times, and it was the worst of times. I am going to tell you just a couple of aspects of it and if you can understand those then you can understand how tough my journey to you has been. I'll tell you about something we all love: Laughter. Laughter, supposedly the best medicine, but sadly not for all.

What could be so delightful, so natural as a baby's laugh? It instinctively just falls from a baby's lips to the joy of its parents. Laughter comes deep from within the body; it comes from the soul. It is like the cleansing water of a mountain brook. Since La Playa I have finally been able to overcome my instinct to cringe at the sound of a stranger's laugh.

Daddy, at la Playa there was never a question of my gender. At La Playa, I was just Violet. There never was a question and there were never any issues. It was not always that way. At the early stages of transition it was painfully obvious to the world what I was going through. One time after going out with a friend to a T friendly bar we decided to go for breakfast at the restaurant across the street. We were both near the same stage of transition, and we were spotted in an instant by other people, especially when we were out together. Onlookers saw us as two gorillas with bad makeup and short dresses.

When the two of us went through the door of the breakfast joint, the place went silent. I mean totally dead silent. Daddy, you could hear the coffee perking and the eggs frying. This silence lasted for a moment, and sometimes a moment can feel like forever. My friend and I took two stools at the counter. Conversation came back in little hushed clumps around the tables. Pointing, soft laughing, we were always at the mercy of peoples' snide hushed comments. Being proud, and being hungry, and also being where we could see the grill, we ordered breakfast. It was always best to see the grill. That way you knew no one was messing with your food. I used to hate restaurants. Because once the waitress figured me out she would be off pointing and whispering to the staff. The staff would take turns coming to the kitchen door and looking. Some of the brave ones would even find chores to do so they could walk by and take a closer look. I always wondered if they were in the kitchen fiddling with my food.

Well, we finished our breakfast, paid and got up to leave. The place went silent again. As soon as we left, the place broke out in laughter. If I was heading into a place and people could see me coming, sometimes I could hear laughter as I came into a place and it would stop when I opened the door. Well that restaurant had a grim end, destroyed when a nearby vacant warehouse was ignited by two homeless people. It was in Worcester, and that fire took the lives of five brave firemen. Daddy, it was so sad. I know from losing you how much the lives of those left behind will be changed. So that spot has memories much sadder than the ones I ever had about it. Life is strange, Daddy. When I was there I would never have believed that anything more painful could ever happen at this spot.

For a long time I hated to be out and hear any laughter for I always thought it had to be people laughing at me. The world had taken something as joyous laughter and used it as a weapon of hurt against me.

Sometimes there was conflict. Daddy, I've had my life threatened by total strangers. I've been punched and tripped several times. In the past I have been made fun of everywhere I went. But also to the credit of humankind, there were more people who wanted to know about me, to help a struggling human, who was plainly and publicly suffering. I have met some wonderful people along the way.

I was lucky with these confrontations when I went out for breakfast after clubbing. And I have to give late night waitresses credit. These late night waitresses are a tough breed. They are the queens of the coffee shops, cross their path and you are out the door. More than once some phobic guy would start. It usually began with a "What the F…" after saying that a few times he was usually standing and getting the waitress' attention. "I can't eat with these freaks here," he would say pointing to my friends and me. A couple of times the waitress would just walk over and remove their plates in the middle of their breakfast and give the loudmouth the bill. It wasn't quite the response they were looking for, and I found it very amusing

Another time a friend and I were waiting for a table at a place in Arlington. It was around 2 am and the place was packed. We had just come from a place in Cambridge called Manray's. Friday night was Goth night and it was a T friendly place. For a while I drifted around a few T friendly clubs as I was safe there. It was cold outside and my friend and I were just inside the door of the restaurant trying to stay warm.

There were three men at a table and one of them went ballistic. He caught the attention of the waitress. "Hey I'm a paying customer and I don't want to eat with those fucking weirdoes".

"Well you won't have to," the waitress snapped back.

She was a pro and she paused for a moment. Her timing was perfect, as a grin was just starting to form on the drunk's face thinking he had won. The waitress finished him off by completing her sentence "You can just leave now before your breakfast comes."

My friend and I gave the drunk a coy smile. We were like two pretty ducks; we just shed his comments like water. Over the last couple years, we had heard it all. After a while it was just a nuisance and there was nothing anyone could say to hurt us.

That drunk grew insane with rage. He was shouting and sputtering, spit flying off his mouth. The waitress pointed to the door, and his friends, who were not as drunk, dragged him out, shouting and cursing the whole way. After he left there was another moment of dead silence. The waitress pointed us towards the drunk's vacated table. We sat and the din of the late breakfast crowd went back to normal.

The late night waitresses loved us. We always lingered after the drunks left and sipped free refills and we always tipped them well for their support. When the greasy spoon got quiet we would chat with them. Somehow they were comfortable enough with us to open up to us about their lives. We would all share our dreams, and our failures. Sometimes we all cried. Those were very tender moments. A late night waitress is not working just because she needs something to do. Her life is not easy.

About 15 minutes later the drunk's friends were back and standing in the doorway. The place was still packed. The waitress looked right at them. "We're not going to have any trouble, boys, are we?" she snapped.

They looked like sheepish boys kicking at the floor. "No, Mam," then a short pause and one of them looked right at us and said "if these ladies don't mind we would like to sit with them."

We had two empty chairs at the table, and we were always ready for the next adventure so we gestured for them to sit. The waitress smiled as she turned back to her chores. The two men sat and immediately apologized for their drunken friend. We chatted. They were curious, so as usual my friend and I shared our struggles with them. People were always surprised our stories were never what they thought they would be. At the end of breakfast they left being allies. My friend and I always felt we would have to win the world over one person at a time.

Sometimes when shopping for clothes, I could often hear and see a couple of women in the next aisle over looking at me and giggling. So Daddy, it was not until La Playa that I could stop hurting every time I walked into, or left, a room and heard laughter. For with time the transition is now complete. I am a woman now. At La Playa, that fact was never questioned.

By the healing shore of La Playa I found the last few missing parts to make me whole -- total acceptance of the woman I am without any doubts. It was so helpful for me at La Playa because back home some people still get it wrong. They don't mean to be, but they are stuck in the past. And their mistakes still cut deep, and hurt every time.

There are lots of ironic and humorous things with all of this. Near the end of transition I had to go to a wedding, and it was demanded that I go as male. But, there was an issue as I no longer had any male dress clothes. So I had to go to the store being a woman and pick out male clothes. Then I had to take them to the ladies dressing room. I had to laugh for this was a twist in my life I had never figured. It made me smile because a few years before I went shopping as male to pick up women's clothes, and would have to take them into the male dressing room. So I'd come a twisted full circle.

The wedding was worse. Everybody stared when I danced with my wife and for the whole evening everyone called me Ma'm. It was the last time I made any attempt to bring back Phil to the public.

At La Playa I could let that last guard down. I no longer cringe when I walk in somewhere and hear the laughing of a stranger. Being able to drop that last guard gave me the final bit of room needed to fully heal. I came down here hurting in body and soul. I had just started to heal when I sent this letter to some friends who belong to a social singles club. Most people in the club do not know about my past, and are unaware of the added dimension to my suffering.

Hi,

It is coming down to just a few precious weeks here in Florida. I actually do not want to come back but the summers down here are hotter than I want to bear. Florida has been very good for me. It is my fist ever sabbatical and I just don't want it to stop. I have regained the use of my knees. I have joined Curves and am losing weight and inches. I bet my blood pressure and cholesterol have been improving. I love New England and always will. But I am older and certain aspects of it, specifically winter, are just too much for my body to take anymore.

I will be back on the Ides of March (15) and am looking forward to seeing all my friends at the SSC. Maybe we can all get together at Scuppers or something when I get back. You all have become very dear to me. Even more so now that I have been away and have seen the loving responses from you all. One is very lucky to have such friends.

The last few years have been very traumatic. Divorce, selling my house, moving, the loss of my pets, the loss of friends and most important and traumatic, was the loss of my family. Somehow being somewhere else has helped to lessen some of that. It has given me a chance to take a few breaths and recover a bit. It is hard to walk the woods where I once walked my dogs and not feel a great loss. One of the first jobs I have to do when I get back is to lay out a waterline and pump station in the West Groton town forest, a place that my dogs and I would run to when the world was closing in on me. It is hard to drive by the house I just sold and remember all the love and good times and wonder what went wrong.

To be down here in Florida was kind of a rebirth to not see items daily that bring back devastating memories. Those of you who know me, know how hard driven I am. I do not like to fail at anything I try. So to daily see things that remind me of my failed marriage and life was not good. To be away has given me a break and a chance to have the time to view things from a distance and regain perspective.

So it is with mixed emotions that I face the time to return. I miss my beloved friends and my precious New England but I do not miss the vestiges of a life that I had tried so hard to make work but failed. Yet none of it really was my fault. I was fighting an impossible fight with the NASA mindset that failure was not an option when in reality failure was the only option. I do not relay this to you all for sympathy but more so you can understand just how healing this trip has been for me.

So don't worry my friends I am truly okay, and will be returning soon. I am a very emotional woman and just need some space and time to rediscover some of the lost threads of my life, and pull a few things together. My emotions run very very deep and it takes me a long time to heal from some things. But healing I am.

So see you soon.

Much Love to you all,

Violet Rose

And Daddy, after purging these feelings I felt great, and my creative ability to write had come back. I was witness to an incident in Ft. Lauderdale that showed how happy and in tune with my surroundings I had become. I want to share a short story with you, Daddy, that I wrote. I feel I am complete now. There are worlds within worlds within worlds. All we have to do is look. A lifetime of experience can be lived in a moment. And it has brought me back to the concept of the woods, and how everything is somehow connected into the same flow. And just like the plants and trees, our lives feed the lives of others. Whether we know it or not the flow is constant around us. This was the first real story I wrote in almost forty years. It was the first time in my life that I wanted to take a moment in time and freeze it in words forever. To have, to keep, to read and remember even when memories fail. So I will read the story to you, as it is important to me for it was when I began really feeling connected to the world again.

Ft. Lauderdale

When I swung the truck around I saw him out of the corner of my eye. He looked like a tourist with his wheeled suitcase. It was not really his looks but the fact that he didn't seem to be going anywhere that caught my attention. I parked the truck in front of the Laundromat and took in the sack of wet beach and travel clothes and dumped them into the washer. While the machine plugged away at the clothes I went outside and sat in the sun. Ahh, the warm Ft. Lauderdale sun. The Laundromat was right off the main strip, and I could see the beach from where I sat. It was two days after Christmas and it was a blessing to be away from the New England winter.

Then I noticed him again. This time he was heading my way, the wheels of his suitcase making an uneven noise as he walked towards me. He had a bad leg and walked with a pronounced limp. He limped up to me and stopped. His clothes were a little worn and my first impression was that he was not a tourist. "Good morning, Mam." He talked in a slow comfortable manner. He saw me get out of the truck so he knew I was from Massachusetts and he inquired as to what brought me so far south. Not wanting to get into the details of it, I just said I was visiting with friends. Then he started talking about himself, and that he had come down from the Midwest because it was warm here. That he had worked mostly in the day labor force until his leg gave out.

Now I could see that the tap was coming soon. I don't know if it was a sadistic streak or if I was just bored. But I knew the next words he said would be the tap. So before he could speak I started in about how I sympathized with him because I was down in Florida for three months trying to avoid the cold that had been ravaging my arthritic knees for the past few winters, and how I could no longer work like I used to either. This distraction worked, and the conversation went on for several more minutes.

Then it finally came "Mam, you seem like a nice lady, could you help a guy out who's down on his luck. Anything would be greatly appreciated." I don't know why I felt moved by his story because mostly I never give money to bums. But something about him was a little different. His cloths were worn but were somewhat clean and not tattered. It was 9am and he did not look hung over and his speech was not slurred. It looked as if he had not completely given up on life.

Being at the start of a three-month furlough, and basking in the warmth of the sun had put me in a really mellow mood. I opened the cap on the bed of the truck and reached into the bag attached to the bike that was stored there. I took out a ten and gave it to the man. His eyes lit up when he saw the bill. He took the money and was very thankful, blessing me and thanking me several times. Then down the sidewalk he went. The wheels making a rhythmic sound as he gimped off down the sidewalk. Fast, then slow, fast then slow until he was out of sight. I figured that was the last of him and the ten that I would see.

The next morning I was at the end of the very same road having breakfast at a table on the sidewalk at a cafe across from Ft. Lauderdale beach. It was a beautiful morning. The sky was clear and the sun was very bright. I had my bicycle propped against the chair next to me. The breeze was gentle and the seas almost calm. Several large ships were anchored off shore, large dark objects on a sparkling sea. I turned and looked up just in time to see the same man standing at the table, and smiling at me. He nodded. "Good morning Mam. How are you this morning?" Our eyes met for a moment. " I just wanted to thanks again. May God bless you." I decided that I was not going to give him anymore money but because he had seemed very polite and grateful, I decided I would get him breakfast. But before I could ask he was off down the sidewalk.

I was intrigued as to why he did not ask for more money. Was it pride or did he know he would not get any more cash. I couldn't tell. But for some reason it gave me respect for him. The day before, he had not come up and simply asked for money as many do. He had limped up and took the time to talk, time to get to know each other and to share aspects of each other's life. He had not begged or whined about how life had given him a bum rap. Today I was totally blown away by the fact that he did not ask for more money. He had found his mark yesterday and generally someone like that would hit the mark again, hoping for another score.

The traffic was light and he crossed the road to the beach, still dragging the suitcase behind him, the wheels still making their uneven rhythmic sound as he crossed. When he was across the street on the beach, he reached inside his suitcase and took out the remains of a loaf of bread. I smiled -- he must have had a good night with the best bread, baloney and wine a ten spot could buy. I hoped that part of my ten had bought the bread that he was generously feeding to the birds.

The sun burned brightly behind him. Thousands of mirrors reflecting the sun glittered on the gentle waves. It was hard to see him through the glare. But there he was, a dark silhouette against the bright sky, holding his hand upward feeding the gulls. His worn and sagging body looking like a cardboard cut-out against the bright sky and glimmering water. The gulls took the bread right from his hand. There was a huge flock of them around him squawking. It brought back memories of sitting on the back of our boat years ago cleaning fish and throwing the remains overboard. When a flock of gulls get together and get really excited their cries make a funny noise. They sound like they are calling "look out, look out, look out." I had to laugh at them when aboard our boat.

There were the gulls swarming around him, and I could hear the familiar cry again, "look out, look out, look out." The cries of the gulls stirred old and pleasant memories. Also it somehow was a moving sight for me that someone with nothing still had something to give -- that the beggars of the ocean were being fed by a beggar of the land. I finished my breakfast and headed off for a bike ride. I rode north along the shore. My eyes still tearing from what I had felt a few moments before, the mixture of old memories mixed with this new happening. Also I was feeling full of myself that I had helped someone if only for a day. That by sharing one half of one percent of the funds I had brought down I had made someone happy. It was a small amount, something I would lose or win at a hand of Texas Holdem and not think twice about it.

I rode a few miles north, turned around and rode back. When I passed the café and the spot on the beach he was gone. Part of me was glad for I knew I would not be giving him any money, but another part was sad for I wanted to hear more of his story. I continued back to the hotel to see what activities my friends would like to do that day. I put the bum in the back of my mind and went to having fun with my friends. I felt a slight smugness that I had helped someone, seen the result of my help and had received the gratitude of the one I helped. There it was all neatly packaged, something to be happy about.

This is where life plays games with me, like it has my entire existence. At the end of the week my friend and I were back at the condo that I was renting at La Playa when a TV news item caught my attention. Two homeless men in Ft. Lauderdale were beaten to death on the very same beach where I had sat. They listed the names but not the pictures. I am so bad with names I could not remember his name to know if it was him or not. My spirits sunk. Had my ten spot made him happy and he was still going to the beach and feeding the gulls with the remains of other gifts or was he gone. Had the small amount of money I gave him caused him to be seen enough by those with even less and he became the target of hoodlums. I will never know. The youths who did the deed were caught and said that they did it for fun, because the people they had chosen to beat were useless and it didn't matter. I felt terrible knowing they were wrong

It just seems that life is never content to let me have my self- fulfilling moment.

Daddy, I had fun writing that last piece. It felt so good and right. Perhaps my deep observations of life around me may help others. I think that I want to write more often and keep track of a few more stories of what I see. Below is the last letter I sent north before coming to see you. Before coming to forgive you. I will read it to you as it may help you understand why it has become so important to ask your forgivness

Hi all,

This will be the last e-mail from me until after I get home. I have really appreciated all of your loving support. You have all given me enough loving care that I do not feel alone in this world. I will be back in a matter of days and am looking forward to seeing you all.

This trip down for me was nothing short of a miracle. When I put some mileage between myself and all the things that reminded me of the recent traumas of my life I was able to heal more completely.

I have one last thing to do on the way home, and it is a whopper. I am stopping in the Arlington National Cemetery and go to the grave of my father. He is a decorated war hero. If you only could have a memory for a father you could not ask for more than him. He had distinguished service, several medals; he was a war hero, what a father to be proud of! So why all these years have I hated him? I hated him for what his death did to my mother and me. He died 8 ½ months before I was born, and neither he nor my mother knew I was there in her womb when he died.

I suffered major birth defects that I still fight now because of all the trauma I received while in the womb. It was caused by my mother's grief over his death. Mom suffered long and hard because of his death.

I have come to a point in my life where I have been able to look back and try to make some sense of things. The last thing I have to do for closure is to visit the grave of my father. Twenty years ago I drove to the Arlington National Cemetery and made it as far as the gate. To go all those miles and not have the strength to go a few more hundred feet was heartbreaking. I felt ashamed about myself. But the time was not right. It would not have been right to go to his grave still filled with resentment. At the time I still had not forgiven him.

Now I am at a point that I can let it all go. It was not Daddy's fault he was killed. I'm sure he would have wanted to come back to us if he could. I'm sure he's not happy with how things turned out. I cannot blame my mother for her own destruction after his death. She was so destroyed by his death she fell into the bottle. There were times I felt so alone, so sad. I cannot blame them or myself for these birth defects I received because of the trauma. She did not know about me for almost five months. Because my size was so small at five months, the Navy doctor estimated she was only three months along, and at first the Navy wanted to deny me survivor rights. So at the time of her grief she finds that she is pregnant and that now her honor is in question. How very sad. After all of that how could I hold her to blame? Her life became an ongoing train wreck. It was just one of those things where no one is at fault. There is no one to blame, no one to resent, just a simple twist of fate. I have healed enough to see things differently now and understand that.

In 55 years I have never visited my father's grave. I now need to go to him, and make things right. I need to tell him I'm sorry and ask for his forgiveness. I need to do this for me. I need to do this for him. It is not right for a girl to hate her daddy, especially when he was so brave and was only serving his country at the end. With this last act of forgiveness I can finally forgive myself for hating him and move on from the past. I need to learn to forgive myself for being so wrong in trying to blame him.

Thank you all for helping me to reach this point with your letters of encouragement. My friends, you are all wonderful. See you all in a little bit. Please do not respond to this letter. It will be the last thing I send before I turn off and box the computer. I will not be online until after I get home. I will be at the meeting at Scupper's on Wednesday. Maybe I will see some of you there.

I am okay and just have something to do that should have been done a long time ago. I don't know why I have opened my heart to you all. But I have. Maybe by sharing some of my story it has given me the support to accomplish this difficult task. But maybe by doing so I can find peace in my life. You cannot have a heart full of hate without somehow hating yourself. Hating time is over.

Love
Violet Rose

So Daddy, from now on I just want to be your wide-eyed girl. Daddy, all I want to be is your daughter. I want to receive a Daddy's love that all girls need. So Daddy, I stand here your daughter, asking for your forgiveness and love. And I want to tell you that I forgive you and will carry you in my heart from now on. Like the dragonfly who spends most of her life under water, so I was submerged in a sea of sadness for what could have been. And like the dragonfly I have climbed out of that watery environment to sprout wings and become a beautiful creature of the sun and sky. To fly above the suffering of the deep, dark world in which I lived.

Good-bye, Daddy, I love you and will see you next year on my way to the healing ocean water of La Playa, to the source of all life, the sea. So sailor hang in there. I will do some research and find out where you are. I will see you before I return to La Playa next winter. I'll see you next fall, but for now I leave you with a Rose -- a Violet Rose.

Chapter 12

So with that I rose from the bench. Life was humming around me. I had sat for hours talking to the graves. Jets were taking off from the airport. Every few minutes another one would roar overhead, great thunderous silver birds gleaming in the warm late afternoon sun. The din of their jet turbines would momentarily overpower the cemetery, then moments later, all was back to the hallowed hushed tones. Some of the ornamental trees had white blossoms waving softly in the breeze.

Groups of schoolchildren kept coming to see the changing of the guards. They would start to collect just before the hour and would leave shortly after the ceremony. I walked away toward the gate past an oncoming group of kids. They were trying to get to the last changing of the guard. I had to smile. They were just kids, talking, laughing, trying to run ahead of the teacher.

The teacher reprimanded them. "Quiet. Slow down. You're in a cemetery." The kids slowed down and turned their voices down a notch. It is tough to ask children to be quiet because it is against their nature to keep still but it is good for them to learn values. For that's how our civilization carries on from generation to generation -- values, goals, fears and prejudices pass from parent to child.

In the soft and caressing breeze I got back to the gates just in time to hear the last few notes drifting from the changing of the guards.

The feeling I had for these gates had changed over the past few hours. No longer did they seem like gates that were there to keep me out but gates that were there to welcome my return when I come back. Each step seemed to be lighter as I passed through those gates. The weight I had carried was gone. My steps were lively and free.

I got back into my truck and paused for thought. What a hard journey it had been. From conception until this moment had been a journey of a trillion tears. And now, even after all those years, the miracle of finding myself only set me off on a whole new journey -- a trip into the T world, and what a strange journey that was.

After I finally accepted myself, life was thrilling for a while. It was as if I had been a prisoner in a castle somewhere and just got a full pardon. It was like seeing the light and hearing the birds for the first time. Everything felt sweet and new with fresh life. The feeling was intoxicating. I was free to be me. It had to be like the dragonfly, a life spent in the dark, under water, and then to be set free to the sky and the light.

But life around me was in full throttle mode to stop this transformation. My family, of course, was devastated. My friends went running off screaming into the night. Employees at work were having issues and quitting. The plateau of success and family I had achieved was falling down in ruins. I had to watch it all happen. I had to experience the pain of those I had hurt around me. I'd go through the pain of a thousand reassignment surgeries than go through that pain of hurting those I loved. But I had to do it. For what was standing proud when everything else crumbled to the ground was me. The real me, the inner core, the light that had given me the strength to carry on. To thine own self be true. For once in my life I had to be true to me. I was being suffocated by life when I finally figured it out.

The fortunate thing for me was that I chose to find help rather than end it all. I had thought about it all the time. Almost every bridge abutment I saw I would analyze to see if it would be possible or not. I already had a list in my mind of sites on route 495 that would do the trick. It would have been so easy late one night, just a flick of the wrist and the pain would be over and I could drive off into the night sky. Free to pick a star and go to it and visit a world that had to be better than mine.

Every time I would turn the wheel towards one of those abutments, at the last possible instant, that inner core of pure light would turn the wheel back, causing the vehicle to careen back on to the road and I would fight to regain control. I did not want to wreck the vehicle and just get hurt. That would be stupid.

If I wasn't going to kill myself then I needed help. For like the dragonfly, once I saw the light of the sky I could not go back. Here's another analogy from nature. Every year a snake sheds its skin. Then the snake goes through a growth phase. After shedding that skin the snake could never go back and fit back into that old skin for two reasons. First, the snake went through a growth phase and now the skin is now too small to put back on. The second, and most important reason, is that the skin is now dead. If the snake tried to put the skin back on the dead skin would kill the snake.

That's a visual of how it was for me. Once I cast off that skin of maleness I had fabricated, the emotional growth phase was phenomenal. I grew so much as a person that I could never put the skin of maleness back on. And like the snakeskin, that skin of maleness was also dead and it would have killed me to put it back on for it would extinguish the inner light. There would be no one to turn the wheel back on some bleak starless night and my soul would be trapped in this hell forever.

Now that I had let my life be run by that inner light I rediscovered the energy flows that surround us. I knew it at one time from the continuity of observing the life forms, and seeing how the positive existence of something gave positive life to the things around it. The bird's joyful songs comes from the branches, where the bird came from a nest in the tree where it was hatched by another bird who lived in the tree. And the tree had roots nourished by the soil kept in place by the plants that depend on the tree's leaves for the nutrients. There were the earthworms that aerate the soil and break down the leaves for the plants to grow to hold the soil in place so the trees can grow to have the branches for the birds to hide. It was a sublime continuity of positive energy of each life form adding to the positive light of life and of the other life forms around it.

I had learned to live in a black hole of negatives. I had learned how to accept all that negative energy, and to wallow in its wretchedness and cling to life with only a tiny shred of hope that someday things would get better. I had learned to expect nothing but pain and misery that, for some reason, was to be my karma in life. I tried to have hope but the life of lies and denial that I was living would see to it that the realization of salvation would never come, that I would live forever in the darkness of that denial. There was only the fact that the inner light which fate or God or some guiding power had put within me would be extinguished without ever seeing the light of day. To go on like that would mean no end of suffering, and I would not have survived.

Some people have told me that what I have done was a brave thing. It was not. It was survival. At first, it was the pure instinct to live, that undeniable force of life that exists in all of us. If you fell overboard from a boat and no one noticed it, and the boat just kept going out of sight, would it be brave of you to swim to a nearby shore? You wouldn't swim across the ocean to try and catch the boat. Would swimming to shore be considered brave or an act of self-preservation?

So in that sea of misery I swam toward the only shore that was ever really available to me. That was the shore of self-acceptance. And like a survivor of a sinking boat I put every ounce of my strength into trying to try and reach that beach. When I finally reached the safety of shore, I crawled up onto its sand and collapsed on the beach, and let the healing sun start to mend my broken soul. I had made it. I was saved.

But this new land was full of strange occupants who at first seemed to be like me but over time many turned out to be nothing like me at all. I started off in these support groups that at first was a tremendous benefit. Just finding some support and people who seemed like myself, helped me think that I was not just going mad.

I let my sensors down and accepted everybody as they presented themselves to me. Many of the girls were going along the same route as me but at the same time there was a large group of people that I did not understand. There was quite a wide range of characters.

At first I began to go to gay and lesbian nightclubs and functions, but soon I noticed that there were subgroups in this new community. Right away the gay community was only mildly interested in my existence. I was on my way to being a complete woman and they were interested in men. There was some support from the lesbian community, and that did help, but there were always the militant ones that felt that if you weren't born a woman that you could never be a woman. Some of it made about as much sense as the backwoods Maine notion that a person could be born and raised in Maine, but because their parents weren't from Maine, the long time locals never accepted that person as a local.

Their opinion was that just cause your cat gave birth in the oven don't mean that those kittens are biscuits. Yup! So if your lineage wasn't from Maine then you weren't from Maine regardless of where or how you were born. So if I didn't come into this world a girl, I sure as hell was not going to be able to live there and leave it as a girl. But that opinion is too harsh and not a reality. For if you were born in Maine and stayed in Maine then where the hell else would you be from? Certainly not from a state you never lived in.

So if the inner core of me was female when I was born than that is what I am forever. If I never gave that up, then how could I be anything other than a woman and have enough harmony in my life to live happily?

So where were the voices of support from my group? They were few and far between. When a girl goes full route like me, and has the ability to fade away into the crowd and become invisible, it usually means she has moved somewhere far away and begins a new life. To become invisible, they have to be careful how they associate with any T contact just for their own safety. They are forced to do this for their very survival. They are right in what they do to survive -- it is the system that is wrong.

Then into the midst of all of this comes me. After being a prisoner for so long I just can't stop some things. For one thing I do not now know how to shut up. I'm always sporting a toe or two blown off by something I said before considering the ramifications of what I said rather than the reality of what I said. For even if some things are true and real, you should not verbalize them and say them. But then again people would ask me things and want an honest opinion. How could I let myself fall back into a life of darkness and lies? To lie would be to introduce a negative force into my life again.

My Nana used to say "Oh what a tangled web we weave when we practice to deceive." It may be corny but it's a hundred percent accurate. One lie leads to another. Now you have two lies. Soon you have to make a new lie to cover up the old ones. Now you have to keep up these lies straight because you would not want to tell a new lie that was in conflict with the old lies.

I am not well liked by many in the T community because of my mouth. If you ask me for my opinion, then that's what you get – an honest opinion. I will not lie unless it's absolutely necessary to spare someone's feelings that I really care about. One time at a group meeting I asked a question that hurt a lot of people and left a lot of them angry with me.

I had some questions about people in the T community and the whole journey. I still don't have an answer to it. I now accepted myself as the woman I was but I was getting criticism from some of the girls about the way I acted. I continued to go to the football games and tailgate with some long-time friends. Sure the transition was tough on all of us but some friends survived and so the football tradition continued. I was told by some T's that real girls do not go to football games. Yet when I went to the games at least twenty-five percent were women, and they seemed to have a great time. And, enough women go to the Patriot's games to ensure there is always a long wait at the ladies room.

I continued working outside at my survey construction-related job and was told by some in the T community that real women don't work in construction. Yet more and more, I see them there. My exposure to the T community turned into a continuous litany of real girls don't do this and real girls don't do that. As best as I could tell in life, real girls go wherever the hell they want and do whatever interests them. That's what makes them real women.

So the question I asked at a group meeting, and which I still wonder about today, is: If you spend all your time analyzing what a real girl does; and you only do what you think a real girl would do; and only act and talk the way you think a real girl would act and talk; are you really just a man trying to play the role of a woman? That if you were a real woman, wouldn't you just simply live your life and do what you liked? And that if you were a real woman, wouldn't you know this? Well, all hell broke loose in the meeting because some of the girls were living their lives that way. Were it not for the therapist, they would have thrown me out. That's how unpopular my question was. It was an honest question as it was something I was trying to put into perspective as far as my journey went. Once I was able to accept myself there was never any question in my mind as to what I was, and I lived an honest and open life.

I was transitioning in a construction-related job in a small New England town. I wore my heart on my sleeve like some dime novel for the world to read. There could never be any more darkness or any more lies in my life, ever again. For all that darkness and evil had eaten away at my life and I just can't deal with the tangled web any longer. There can be no more striving to deceive.

I stirred up more anger at another meeting with this question: What about the T who goes out to clubs dressed as a woman to gain the confidence of a woman and have an advantage? What about this T who is ready to exploit the openness of female-to-female conversations because women let down their guard around other women. Now if a T is telling these woman about the struggles of the T life, but their real motivation is to get a woman into bed for sex in the traditional male to female manner, does that not make the T a man? Or, even worse, a sexual predator? Because the only reason the T does it is for the attention and the sexual gratification of male to female sex with a little transvestite twist.

Long before I could possibly accept myself, I stopped having any interest in trying to be a man. I gradually slipped into androgyny and stayed away from any form of intimacy.

Those two questions ensured that I was somewhat drummed out of the T- corps, and that I was to become isolated there, set apart as too different than the rest of the herd. But having set myself free to think for myself, I needed answers to these two questions. I needed it for me. I also met people who were fetish cross-dressers, who dressed in women's clothing for sexual gratification. Those I had no trouble seeing as men.

There was another group of the T community that made my journey tougher than it needed to be, and that was drag queens. I had many lesbians confide in me just how much they hated them, and how drag queens actually made it harder for them to accept someone like me. Drag queens are men who dress as women for attention. Often times they are performers. Their makeup and outfits are always outlandish. Those of them that were performers and worked in clubs got a lot of their laughs at the expense of women. Lesbians typically hated them for this and very rarely find them funny.

Exhibitionists made up another sub-group within the T community. They dressed in similar over-the-top fashion as the drag queens, and always had to be the center of attention. They would go out in public in clothes only appropriate for the red light district. They lived for the attention.

Of course, they all have the right to pursue happiness however they want. I am not judging or condemning any of them. All I am saying is that from my perspective, as one trying to gain acceptance for who I am, I don't understand these behaviors. But these people are more visible to the general public and continue to make it difficult for people to understand the road that I had to take. I am not trying to scold anyone, but just trying to explain how the whole thing affected me.

So I found out that not only was I a member of a small group of individuals with gender identity disorder, but that when I entered this small group, in reality, I only belonged within an even smaller sub-group. It all was beginning to feel a little too restraining, a little too confining. According to some in the T community I had to watch what I do, watch what I say. It was all just beginning to look like another role to play and my acting days are over forever.

I made my way along the scary road. My ability to connect with people at a very deep level helped me to identify the shallow people and the deeply disturbed, and I avoided all of them because they were a danger to me. They were a direct link back to the life of lies I had before letting out that inner light. They were a link to the dark days.

My instincts worked well as the people I found that I was safe with were an inspiration to me. When I found someone I could trust then I would unburden my soul in hopes that they could help me. That maybe with their help they could help me lighten the load or at least adjust it so it did not hurt so much. And slowly but surely it worked. There were shoulders to cry on. People who might not totally understand but were nonetheless very compassionate.

The more I walked in the light of truth the more people I met along the way. For now I was out of the T community and walking the road of life sharing my soul with people who were suffering with other issues in life besides gender. I found that by sharing my light, my inner core, with them that the honesty that I was trying to exemplify would inspire them with issues in their life and help lessen the burden they carry. It was really inspiring. The more I walked in the light the more hands emerged from within the light to help me further along. Sometimes the light was so bright I could not see the faces. But every hand I had the strength to touch someone they carried me yet one more step along the road. So if I could keep the strength to keep going, then every time I fell, there was a helping hand up. So with that I would gather up my burden and continue. Sometimes I staggered, sometimes I fell, a lot of times I got hurt in the fall. But I kept my dignity and got up. If I was always a lady and always trying, there was always a hand to help me.

Just like the nurses in the hospital, if I at least tried to head in the right direction there was someone to help and hold me and get me there. To help me into the light of honesty and respect and to help my true light heal all the wounds of the journey; to help me shower in the light of my inner soul and wash all the mistakes away.

Now many of my emotional wounds are healed. Some healed completely and some are scarred. Some still fester even in the light of day and will take longer to heal. But healing is a step-by-step process that takes time.

I have discovered some real joys and my life has been rewarding. Everything I tried to do using the male amour that I fabricated ended in failure. Now after finding my true self, almost everything leads to success. The difference lies in communication. You cannot effectively communicate with the world if you are not honest with yourself. Also, if you live in a castle at the base of a mountain then you isolate yourself from any help that might be there for you. Nobody will ever know what you are going through.

So with my new communication skills maybe I should start to move away from construction and try something different. I should tell my story of salvation to someone. Maybe I should try being….. a writer.

Chapter 13

So I sat in the truck for a long time and thought about how tough the journey had been. Sometimes it makes me sad about how little the average person knows about someone like myself. I was not gay, and other than being raped, never had any sexual contact with men. I lived a life of extreme danger and denial for a long time. My life was hell because of it. There were times when I had fun and thought I had control of my life but mostly my life just felt like a hollow existence. At first I did not know what was wrong but I did know that something was not right. I did not seem to have the same perceptions of life as the boys around me. Somehow I saw life in a more delicate way than they did, particularly between the ages of five until the time I got raped. Some of the clothes that I insisted on wearing at that age were actually from the girls section of the store but were always just androgynous enough to be acceptable for a young boy.

I loved to wear long flowing oversized male shirts and tight Capri pants called clam diggers. I liked how it felt to walk with the shirt flowing with me. I still remember that feeling of being at peace when dressed like that. At that time I had traditional male clothing for school, and then I had my after-school clothes. I always liked my after-school clothes best.

Being raped set me off on a lifelong quest to bury that soft side and to get tough in order to survive. It was a lifelong quest to be a man, and I pursued one dangerous thing right after another. For a time, it was endless immersion in alcohol, 12-16 drinks everyday for years on end, to quench a thirst that no amount of liquid could drown. I thought I was in control of the alcohol because I would only drink in afternoons and evenings during the workweek. Weekends were a different thing, and my drinking would usually begin before noon on my days off.

Weekday mornings were the worst. Sometimes I would not get in until 4am from drinking with the boys and then would have to get up at 6am and go to work. I did well at work though because I worked very hard and kept my mind occupied. So between working hard and drinking hard I never gave my mind the time to think about anything except those two tasks.

After the age of ten, I started studying the ways of boys and men. I had to fit in. I had to -- after all I was a boy. When I took off my clothes I looked like one, so why did I seem to see things differently than other boys? Why did it seem like I experienced things differently. Even after being raped, I could not control myself enough to stay out of my mother's closet. As her bipolar condition got worse it gave me more access to her closet. When she passed out on the couch, it gave me some time to play. The best was when she went next door to drink with a friend. She would be gone all afternoon, and I had time to try on several outfits.

The first complete girl's outfit I wore was at my cousin's house. She was 14 and I was 8. My cousin and I were up in her room goofing around. She had just gotten on the JV cheerleading squad and had a cute new uniform. It was beautiful -- short skirt, matching panties, sweater with a letter on it. She knew I was somehow softer than most boys, and before long I could hardly believe my ears when she asked me if I wanted to try on the outfit. God that was exactly what I had wanted. I had the uniform on in a very short time. Then she showed me her cheers. I learned them all in a heartbeat and we were up in her room jumping and doing cheers when a call came up the stairs.

"What are you kids doing?" my aunt shouted upstairs

"Just doing some cheerleader cheers" replied my cousin

We went back to doing cheers and did not hear the creaky stairs. Suddenly the door swung open and my mother and aunt stood there. Their faces were incredulous, and then anger filled my mothers face. "Get out of that stuff. We're going home!"

My cousin just stood there toeing the floor. So I quickly took the uniform off and put on my own clothes. It being the weekend, I was wearing my long shirt and clam diggers. We went a few streets away to our house. It was that summer we were building the house in Littleton. I don't think my mother talked about it much. I think she knew I was a little different than the other boys. After all she was the one coming home with the Capri pants for me. No other boy wore them.

This was during the 1950's and there never was any mention of such things as gender identity disorder. At that time in my life, I had room for self-expression so I did not notice my gender disorder for I was allowed to look how I felt. I loved the feeling of clothes that flowed when you walk. I would walk and run in the yard, my oversize shirts gracefully swaying with my movement.

Two things changed my life in a big way. One was being raped. I never wanted to have that happen again. I had my clam diggers and flowing shirt on when it happened. My attackers had told me how pretty I was. It really was a brutal attack on my femininity. After that, I purged all my Capri pants and long shirts from my wardrobe. I saw them as the reason for being raped. At that moment I hated all those clothes. I tried to bury my femininity but it kept coming back.

Periodically I would sneak into my mother's closet to try on more and more of her clothes, right down to a stuffed bra and girdle with the little clips for stockings. I had my own precious pair of stockings I had stolen from her. I kept them washed and hidden in my bedroom. When I was dressed as a girl I had such feelings of contentment. I felt at one with myself.

The second thing that really changed my life was testosterone. It is very powerful. I have seen experiments with rats where they inject testosterone into female rats and the females then take on male behavior, fighting among themselves and even trying to mount other female rats. Once I had all that male testosterone pumping through my veins, it changed me tremendously. It was at this time that I stopped having those dreams of being taken somewhere and being changed into a girl. After that I started having no dreams at all.

Muscles became easy to build up by exercise. The testosterone drive overwhelmed everything else. My body was awash in it. Now I buried that feminine side really deep. After the age of seventeen I was able to bury that feminine part of me very deep in my mind. I put it away with my memories of childhood, but there was still room in that dark space where I would hide the things that I did not want to deal with. But even with testosterone it somehow just seemed like a temporary patch to an existing condition. I felt different than the men around me. I had a normal sex drive but when all the guys would ogle a woman and want to be with that woman, I instead would look at the woman and want to be her. It was weird, because here I had developed into a rough tough guy exterior, so how could I want to be her? Whenever it happened I managed to just stick it away with the rest of the stuff in my mind.

There was no slipping back towards femininity until about the age of 25. Then I started having that serial dream of being chased by some unknown pursuer, the dream of running through a dying landscape dragging my family along. What has been strange for me is that in those dreams I never had any gender. We were always running so hard, escape was all we could think about.

A few months after the dream came back, I found myself one day putting on my wife's clothes. I became very ashamed and immediately took them off and tried to purge the whole memory. Stuff it back into that place -- that place in the back of my mind was starting to get quite full. After that I turned to vicious hard work during the day and pounding down countless beers after work. Along with drinking I started abusing drugs by smoking lots of pot. I habitually smoked at work. I had little hit pipes that contained enough for one puff of weed. We worked in the woods and there were times when I would be a couple hundred feet from my assistant so it was easy to step behind a tree and take a hit or two and then just go back to work smiling. The guys liked working with me. I ran things in a laid back friendly way but always produced more work and of a better quality than all the other crews.

I was building up the respect of all those around me. They saw a big burly guy with a beard, strong as an ox, hard working during the day and beer guzzling with the boys at night. By the time I got home everyday, I was fully drunk. If I did not go out with the boys then I would buy a six pack and drink three during the half-hour ride home. I always had cases of beer at home. I used to love the fall when I could get up from the couch and the warmth of the wood stove, and go out to the back porch where the cases of beer were stacked, and get an ice-cold beer chilled by Mother Nature. I kept them there year-round until it got so the weather was so cold they were in danger of freezing, and then I would keep the beer in the house.

For a long time I kept things in check by simply anesthetizing myself. In my mind I knew I was hiding from something but I simply did not let myself think about it. Because of this, my life seemed hollow.

Because it seemed like I achieved anything I set my sights on, I worked on my career and would pick goals to reach. Eventually I would reach that goal and be happy for a while but then would get bored and set off on some new goal. My life should have been happy but somewhere underneath something was still wrong. I had absolutely no fear of death. I routinely took death-defying risks and loved that feeling of being on the edge. For a while that was what I lived for.

At about the age of about 30, the urge to dress in woman's clothes returned. As hard as I would fight it, I could not stop it. Afterwards, I was ashamed and would purge the incident. I'd go back to several months of extremely dangerous behavior to convince everyone of my manliness. The world never questioned it. For the world saw me as a tough wild man, living a super manly existence. Trouble is somehow I could never believe it. Now matter how wild the stunt, something was wrong. There was always that initial rush of cheating death but then when that settled down I always went back to that hollow feeling. Just like when I worked on the steel, at the end of the day there was never a spot high enough to climb. I could never find a spot that was high enough to escape the world of confusion in which I lived.

When I was 40, I got hooked on snowmobiles. I could go out in the woods behind my house and could ride to New Hampshire's international snowmobile trails. There were never any fish and game officers in the places where I rode so it was always at full throttle. The trails were narrow and loaded with trees on the sides. I always rode that line of danger and went as fast as possible. The thrill of being on the edge was intoxicating. I could have been killed a thousand times but I never was.

I made a new friend who had a son in his early twenties. The father and son worked together and both of them rode snowmobiles, so we developed a quick and close friendship. I started going up to their camp in NH with them to snowmobile. My friend and his son were big and impressive looking men. The son would have all his friends up to the camp. The son's friends were really rough and tumble. Some of them were Hell's Angels while others were just bar brawlers. All were really big and rough, everyone over 200 pounds and very strong. It was a hulking mob.

We would ride the snowmobiles to bars around the neighboring towns. Rat racing amongst our selves on the way over. It somehow reminded me of the Wild West, with a roughneck crowd of wild men galloping into an innocent town on our stallions of steel. Racing, bumping each other, cranking the throttle at the end of a curve and spinning the track to kick up snow onto the machine behind you. If the temperature was below 20, the machines would love it and run really nice. The foul smell of the two-stroke engine seemed to change and take on a nutty smell. It's hard to explain but it seemed to smell good. So there we were buzzing though the woods. The machines ranged from new sleek fast ones to old crap cans kept running just so the guys could make the bar run. We must have looked like a scene from the Mad Max movies descending on those backwoods bars.

When we went into the bars, we always took control and always outnumbered the locals both in numbers and size. We would take off the outer winter clothes and would just start pounding down booze. When I went to the men's room I always made sure my boots were tied because something always happened. I never understood it. Almost all of the gang, when they used the men's room in these places would go in and just piss on the floor. After a while the urine on the floor would be a quarter inch deep or more. Like dogs marking their territory and making a statement. We were so strong in force that no one every said anything to us about it. That was disgusting, and I could not understand it.

I hung around with these guys for several years, and all the while, things were changing inside me. I could no longer keep the feminine side hidden. I started wearing long sweaters past the hips and women's leggings. I also started clear coating my fingernails. The gang saw it all change slowly with time and mostly did not comment. I was still big and strong, rough and tough, at least on the outside. The last year I rode with these guys became positively surreal. We would ride off to a bar somewhere and walk in. I would have a full beard, usually frozen with ice from riding. Then I would take off my helmet, and nearly waist-long hair would tumble out. I would take the snowmobile suit off to reveal a long pastel sweater and women's leggings.

The gang seemed to accept my strange behavior as just that -- strange. They never really commented to me much about it. Once in awhile, there might be a harmless remark. When we went into the bars, there was always an eye on the lookout for me by someone in our gang. I think the guys somehow liked gender bending as an excuse to look for confrontations with the locals. If anyone dared make a comment to me, there was always some big guy ready to intimidate the person who dared speak. Somehow it all helped bring the feminine side out even more. I started to somehow feel like Ma Barker with a gang who would fight for my honor. The feminine side just kept rushing out. I was at a point in my life where I could no longer hide the fact that I did not belong in the male world, and that I had hid amongst them for so long my soul was weary. Now all those empty victories, all those brushes with death, it all had to go.

This was the point in my life when driving alone I would play chicken with bridge abutments late at night. I would think of different ways to take myself out, and not make it look like suicide so my family could collect the insurance. I figured if I drank enough booze, it would look like I fell asleep at the wheel. It would have worked and I was obsessed with these thoughts. It was at that point when I reached the lowest point of my hollow existence that I finally had to find acceptance in my life.

I accepted my true self. I accepted that I was different than other men. I recognized that my inner soul was that of a woman; that my way of thinking and problem solving was more female than male as best as I could tell. When I accepted myself it was like a true rebirth. My hurting spirit had been set free. My spirit was flying with the dragonflies. My body was a different story altogether. But the miracle of accepting myself was the fact that I now would allow myself to go get help and see what was going on with my life.

Once I accepted the fact that I had to become a woman, there was never any looking back. At first I joined self-help groups. My life was evolving into femininity. The beard was now gone, which was a shock to those around me since I wore it since college. People were surprised because the face hidden beneath was not what they expected. The lines were not square and masculine. The only give-away to being male was a constant beard shadow. Now I had developed to the point when I was outside of the work environment, I was always dressed as a woman and was seeking places where I could go and be safe. Even now my work appearance was totally androgynous and from a distance it was hard to tell my gender.

I was having lots of issues in public. When dressed as a woman people would call me, "he" and when I was dressed as a male people were calling me "she." It was quite confusing and frustrating. One time I was in a men's room, and I was wearing a long sweater and leggings, while standing and peeing in a urinal. A father and son came in, and I heard the boy say to his father. "Look dad, there's a woman standing there peeing." The father whisked the kid into a booth and had a hushed conversation with his son while I washed my hands. I began to live a life of isolation for a while. Transition was grueling.

It was after this time I had an encounter with a news reporter at a planning board meeting. I had long hair and nails, and was presenting projects to town boards. I wore totally androgynous clothing and the world was becoming confused. People in the town were seeing and talking about me being in public as Violet. The reporter told me he wanted to write an article about me. The article would focus on what it must be like to look like I do and work in construction. His timing was almost perfect. I had just accepted the fact that I had to become a woman few months before and had written my family telling them that I needed to be a woman to survive.

I confided in the reporter what was going on in my life and told him that within the next year or so I was going to change my name and begin living full-time as Violet. I told him I would contact him when it was going to happen. By now I had been into therapy sessions for a couple of years and had started down the road toward full transition. By now I was a woman all the time, I just dressed differently for work.

I gave my family my letter of intention and called the reporter. I had two interviews with him, and he wrote an article about Phil becoming Violet and told me when it would run. That day at work my heart kept racing. On the way home I bought the paper and started to look. There on the front page of the second section at the top was the story. It was a hot summer day. By now I had been running my own company in a building behind the house. After the workers went home, I sat on the back steps. The air was hot, humid and still. It almost seemed like I could hear the jungle drums beating out the latest news. I sat there in the stillness listening and thought, what have I done? There is no way back from this. A huge bridge in my life was ablaze.

I never liked burning my bridges, and here I was not only burning the bridges I was crossing, but I was blowing up the abutments so they could never be rebuilt. I had quite a few people in public come up to me and thank me for finally being honest with the world, and now they understood, and what they had seen over the past few years finally made sense. Some people chose to not associate themselves with me anymore, and eventually through time almost all whom I had considered friends had left. For as time went on, the person they had known was disappearing before their eyes. It was more than most people could endure.

I was undergoing very long sessions of electrolysis. At first I would go for several two-hour sessions a week, that entailed hundreds of thousands of little jabs and shocks to my skin. The woman I went to was very good and did excellent work but it was a slow and tedious process. Each hair had to be individually zapped. An electrical probe is slid down inside each follicle and a current run to the probe. The resulting zap was a little worse than feeling a mosquito bite but not quite as bad as a bee sting. Each hair would eventually come back and would need one or two more zaps to finally kill it.

I had tried many laser treatments without results, and settled on the time proven method of electrolysis. It was time consuming and costly. I spent a small fortune on this, basically everything I could extract from my paychecks. My life as a high roller was over. Now I needed every cent for the journey.

Once I began living full time as a woman, I qualified to receive hormones. My therapist followed a method called The Harry Benjamin Standards of Care. It is an advisory policy for caregivers to use when dealing with transitioning people, especially those going from male to female. Most of the T girls resented it as it took a long time and some went so far as to quit therapy and buy hormones from overseas, taking the chance of putting god-knows-what in their veins. These were the same girls who went to Thailand for surgery because the surgeons there are amenable to expediting things rather than adhering to the Benjamin requirements.

If you went to a surgeon in the United States or Canada, you had to adhere to these standards. So I spent about five years going through these steps, and I had made it to the stage where I could get hormones. I had gone through a psychologist in my HMO and he was happy to let me pick a specialist. I had done a lot of research and knew a woman who specialized in Gender Identity Disorder and went to her.

When an endocrinologist gave me a prescription for hormones, the HMO was not surprised and covered the pills with my usual co-pay. I was amazed and delighted. About a month after starting taking the pills I had a terrible reaction. I had hurt my knee dancing in heels at an alternative lifestyle bar. It hurt slightly when I walked but I just kept working and going out at night. It was sore but not too bad. Well, the knee had water on it somewhere and must have gotten infected, and what resulted was a head to foot case of psoriasis patches. I was crushed once again. Everyone in my life said it was the hormones that were killing me. The endo doc told me it must be something else so I kept taking the hormones. Two weeks later the knee went ballistic and swelled to many times its normal size and needed to be drained in the emergency room one night. Several days later I developed cellulites, which is an infection of the soft tissue under the skin. I had it on the side of my face and felt like I was going to die. It was a severe infection and was spreading, my whole face was swelling. One eye was swollen shut.

At this time I was seeing doctors in Worcester, as I did not want to run into someone local in the doctor's office. So now feeling like I was dying, I called a local doctor's office next to the local hospital. He was new and he was looking for patients. I begged the receptionist that

I had to come down because I was dying, and that I needed a local doctor. My wife drove me over and the nurse immediately put me in an examination room. There I was lying in a fetal position shivering and covered with sores. My right eye was swollen shut and the swelling was spreading down my face. I was a mess and in serious trouble. I tried to tell him a little about what I was going through, about the hormones and the Gender Identity Disorder, and I had to pray to God that this doctor would be a credit to his Hippocratic oath and would save my life. For in a very short time I was approaching my demise. If the infection wasn't stopped soon I was going to start having organ and brain damage. Thank God he was true to his oath. I was helped into a wheelchair and sent directly to a hospital room and a bed. That doctor is still my primary care doctor for he saved my life that day. They arranged an IV drip while my wife helped fill out the paper work

The name now on my license was Violet Rose, but the gender was male and in those short hospital johnnies, there is no arguing it genetically. But I kept telling the staff I needed to be referred to as a woman, that it was important. I was really sick and could not argue so the nurse put F/M on my wristband and I just accepted it. I could be a stereo for a few days if it meant surviving.

That whole first day I kept quarreling with the male nurse who was attending me. He kept referring to me as "he" and it hurt every time he did. Later in the afternoon, I told one of the nurses that I needed to see the head nurse. The antibiotics had reduced the swelling around my mouth and throat and I could talk a little better. I told her a little of my struggles and then told her about the male nurse and told her how upset it made me and if I was going to heal I needed peace of mind. Something must have been put on the chart as the night nurses never messed up, and for the next three days the nurse I talked to attended to my needs. By now the psoriasis was beginning to heal, but I was still covered in bright red raw spots that constantly needed cream and itched like crazy. The areas swollen by cellulites were back to being normal.

The nurse called the endo doc and all through this I was allowed to continue taking my hormones. The infection was cured, and I went home three days later. A couple of weeks later when my knee was getting much better and the sores almost gone, I went back to the hospital with flowers and thank-you cards for the nurses. In time I healed completely. I never would have believed it. My face was so swollen I thought that I would never look right again, that I would end up looking like the Hunchback Quasimodo. But through it all I never missed a dose of the hormones.

The hormones, like electrolysis, were long-term treatments. As the beard diminished and the hormones softened my features, the line between male and female began to blur. From day to day there was no perceptual change but over time the changes were massive. I began to pass first with many females who were busy with their lives and never took a second look. Women are usually more accepting than men anyway. So I began to be able to integrate myself in the woman's world and begin to get support from genetic women outside of the T community. Then after a while I could pass with boys and men, and I was on my way to becoming invisible. The hardest scrutiny to pass with was from little girls. They kept nailing me. The last time it happened was years ago on my way down to Provincetown. I was in a store and there was a mother and young daughter behind me in line. The daughter looked up at me and said "Are you a man?"

I was caught off guard but managed a giggle. I looked at the girl and said "No, I'm not. Are you a little boy?"

She giggled and coyly said "No, I'm a girl"

"So am I" I replied and looked at the mother who was embarrassed.

"Of course she's not a man" the mother told the child. The cashier was amused and I do not believe that either woman read me as a man. That was the last time that happened, and now I am never spotted by observant little girls.

The transition at work was agony at first. The wrong gender was always used, but I found a clever way of dealing with the issue. I had a coffee can covered in pink paper. Instead of getting mad at people, which only made them more dysfunctional, I established a fine of 25 cents if someone used the wrong gender in addressing me. I let it be known that the fund was going toward surgery, and when someone messed up I always made them put a quarter in the can.

After that even the worst offender never got much above a buck in fines before he figured it out, and addressed me with the proper gender. It was a non-confrontational way of dealing with the issue. My therapist liked the idea so much, she passed it along to the other girls she helped.

I had finally met the requirements to be able to schedule surgery. One of the stipulations of the Benjamin standards was that I had to live 24/7 as a woman in every respect, including using the ladies room. This is where T's are the most vulnerable both to physical violence and legal issues. It is against the law for a man to use a ladies' room. Until after surgery, we are legally and anatomically male. As such I could be subject to arrest and could have been subject to being a sex crime offender.

But, if I used the men's room, I ran the risk of getting beaten up or killed by some phobic guy. So it was always a damned if you do, and damned if you don't situation. Once I went 24/7 my preparation had been enough that I was always able to use the ladies' room without a hitch. Fear kept those visits quick when I had to go.

I booked a surgeon and it was an eighteen-month wait. By then any ties with my old identity and life had been removed. I had continued to run a business and deal with all the issues of transition in a small town. It had been a continuous struggle. It had seemed to be taking forever. These standards of care really keep the clock running slow. I understand now why. Because before surgery I had to be dead certain that this is right for me, and that I had to live in a woman's world long enough to see if it would work. Many girls do not pass well enough and find the year of 24/7 too much to be able to do. Some girls at that point go back to living dual lives or even go into denial and back to male.

The saddest situation for a T girl to be in is to be able to go on, but not have the money to do so. Many girls when they come out lose their jobs and then have trouble finding work. Many have very troubled lives. Almost 98 percent of the marriages end in divorce. The T community lives a life of endless suffering of such huge proportions that the outside world cannot even imagine how bad it is.

The Benjamin standards of care were in place also to prevent the unforgivable act of surgery that proved to be the wrong solution, because once it's done, it cannot be undone.

It seemed as if slowly the days to surgery ticked by, and then suddenly it was time to go. I went to Portland, Oregon and had my date with destiny. It was agonizing, and took a long time to get over. My wife true to her word stayed until after surgery and divorced me. We went to divorce court together. The judge called XXX vs. XXX, and my wife and I went up before the judge. The judge was looking around for Mr. XXX when I spoke up and said I used to be Mr. XXX. He seemed to just take it in stride and the divorce was granted. A marriage of 32 years had ended. We parted in life both broken hearted in our own ways. It was very tragic and we had both suffered greatly.

The last few years have been bearable. My life is as good as it can be in my situation. I have all new friends, most of whom do not know my story. I have a good life where I live but there are many dangers. Too many people know me and my past, and keep outing me to new friends that I make. I do not tell people up front about my journey as it makes it too tough to be able to live. I just want a life like any other woman and not an ongoing soap opera.

One choice I had to make when I chose to go down this road is that I may have to spend the rest of my life alone. I would like to be with a man but am afraid to date. I can't out myself to every Joe I meet, and I don't feel safe dating and not telling. T girls get killed sometimes by male lovers who discover their past and freak out. So men are dangerous to me and I just chose to live alone. After all the suffering in my life I am content to just be left alone, even though I know firsthand the joys and advantages of being married.

The trouble with where I live and work is that it's too close to my new friends that I have found in the social singles club, and I fear my identity could be revealed at any time. It is uncomfortable for me always worrying about detection. When I was in Florida, I was far enough away to feel safe for the first time in my life and it was intoxicating. I healed more down there from my wounds than I ever imagined. I now know I may need to move away from Massachusetts to finally complete this journey. Also I feel that my story is too compelling not to tell the world.

So to my current friends who didn't know my story, I want you to know that I have drunk from your well of friendship as a woman who was parched and had previously only known an arid existence. I cherished every cup of friendship as if it were the last, because knowing that eventually you will all learn my story has made it so bittersweet. But my story is too compelling not to tell. So if I need to relocate one more time, then so be it. For those of you who feel tricked and are angry, I did only what I had to do to survive. For those of you who are forgiving and accepting, and stayed to offer support -- welcome to my world. I love you all now more than before as I have finally learned to love myself.

Printed in the United States
88769LV00005B/301-348/A

9 781434 332332